I0416589

DOWN WITH UP AND UP WITH DOWN

(With neither common sense nor God?)

by

Foster Archer

authorHOUSE

1663 LIBERTY DRIVE, SUITE 200
BLOOMINGTON, INDIANA 47403
(800) 839-8640
www.authorhouse.com

© 2004 Foster Archer
All Rights Reserved.

No part of this book may be reproduced, stored in a retrieval system, or transmitted by any means without the written permission of the author.

First published by AuthorHouse 08/10/04

ISBN: 1-4184-3063-3 (e)
ISBN: 1-4184-3061-7 (sc)
ISBN: 1-4184-3062-5 (dj)

Printed in the United States of America
Bloomington, Indiana

This book is printed on acid-free paper.

CREDITS

With gratitude to Virginia Ruby for her patient recording of the manuscript. And to Libby Archer for her insistence that I stop making changes and finish the work....or else..... For in truth I am not sure that I ever could have finished it without their interest.

FOREWORD

This small book is the condensed gathering of my ninety-four years of closely observing and questioning life. My general assessment is that we are being led blindly into personal and therefore national disaster. And it does not have to be!

In my near century of life, I have seen incredible accomplishments of engineered materialism. And I have seen the spirit of our people brushed aside to make room for the ever expanding demands of the hideously rich dominators. Our whole system of life is directed and herded toward the insane greed of the dominating elite. And it does not have to be!

We are now become a nation hated and feared above all nations. And rightly so. And more vulnerable to attack and defeat than any other nation. And this does not have to be!

Certain basic realities need to be established in order to bring our country into the degree of safety and purpose and health to which we all are entitled. And I make no single exception when I say that each of us is entitled to basic equality. We are God created individuals and only by recognizing this truth, and then treating it wisely and justly can we be worthy of the national excellence which seems most vital.

One. There has been a century of regression from a state of God acceptance and trust. We are no longer persuaded toward acceptance of God by the efforts of Religions and their advocates. We need to know, outright and unequivically if there is indeed God Creator of All or is there not. To many of us, this is vital. I strove long to find this proof and yet it was there so plain and available that it still shames me.

We need a true Democracy. This means a literal voting voice by every qualified voter. And it is for the first time available.

We need to restructure our ambitions from the drive for more and more, to the enjoyment of less and less. This will result in greatly lessening the stress under which we live. And when all needful labors are divided among all available workers we will at last have full employment with greatly reduced working hours.

We must gradually convert from vast centralized industries to small localized industries and this will greatly reduce the need for auto travel and will return us toward the slower and safer village life wherein every family can have a garden. At present we live, the entire nation, at the mercy of truck lines which are extremely vulnerable. Not a pleasant thought.

We need a new Money. The only sound support of money has, from the beginning of barter, been the backing of labor. This is a universal base of value unchanging whether in the building of a pyramid or the building of our home. There is no fluctuation, depression or wild inflation possible in labor backed money. And it gives any country the means to carry out large projects without one cent of debt.

We surely must abolish our potitical 'system'. Utterly wipe out career politics and the two opposing teams vying for personal gains. Viewed calmly this is simply disgraceful.

There must be one common income. No matter what the labor may be. A just employment would soon evolve. Partly by rotation and partly by hours of employment. No person shall be penalized, granted less than a standard wage, and no person shall be granted an income above the mean. Yes, this can be made to work.

There will be no profit under any circumstance. No fortunes shall be permitted to build. Any income above the mean will be confiscated for taxes. All taxes shall be devised and shared by majority decision.

We shall be a People, Self Regulating. The creed of judging worth by money and prize will be abolished. We live now in a system of competition, and it is destructive and demeaning. We must learn the opposite, cooperation. For by so doing, we live in an advanced state of human development and thus we shall become a people no longer hated and feared, but rather a people honored and loved. All this, and more, is now available.

TABLE OF CONTENTS

INTRODUCTION

Introductions tend to bore, especially if they're not by the writer. If the writer actually wrote it, let him face the reader and hope for mercy.

I'm an Old Guy who aimed at writing this book most all my life. You may respond with 'so what? a long time of wanting to do something is not rare.' Too true. But if that long life centers the observance on the rampant stupidity evident in almost everyone, plus the full evidence of one's own stupidity, then the result can be a working grade of wisdom. Wisdom to see the humor and beauty of it all; and the strange offer of a truly unfettered life shared in Joy. I say Joy, because a fitting term is beyond words and beyond thought. So, working with what is left of this grand country, let's ponder our future. Ah so.

It was unlike any other century, that Twentieth. It was explosive. More energy of change was released than in all combined history of mankind.

Forces which had slumbered and dreamed were now awakened and joined in the purpose of altering the very nature of human thought and existence. New trends began softly and slowly, as a great freight train starts, and gaining speed and power soon were roaring over the lands and nothing dare stand against them. So were born the trends that hurtled into this new age and they have the power and will to utterly destroy our world. In that last century we went from hand-to-mouth culture to a machine-to-mouth culture and are determined to mechanize and automate every last function of life short of sex.

With the expressed purpose of enslaving mechanisms to the needs of humanity we have rather become ourselves enslaved to the machines.

In the process of this overall revolution, we have gained some things and lost some things. But the price we pay now, and shall soon pay far more heavily, has been a very bad overall exchange. It seems that we humans, given choices to make between things beneficial, and things harmful, will make every effort to prove the wrong thing is better than the right thing. We will invent marvelous concoctions and use them to our own detriment.

I've been closely observing life throughout most all of the past century and now on into this one, having been born in January of 1910. That was just six years after the Wright Brothers goosed their contraption of flight on the sands of Kitty Hawk in North Carolina and the cratelike bird gave a nervous leap which carried it a measurable space and they repeated that several times and called it 'flight'.

Flight, like the birds, surely made Adam and Eve gaze upward from time to time. Such efforts had been made in fact and fiction down through all the centuries of history. Then, in this one century, the idea was jelled and just about twenty years later they flew across the ocean! Isn't that astounding?

And then there was the matter of the moon. How many a bumbling youth and maid had held hands and gazed up at the mystery of the moon, squinting to see its face, letting it speak the words of love which they could not.

Sixty years after Kitty Hawk, a rocket propelled men up to that mysterious orb and they jumped out and kicked the dirt and jumped about on that moon face, left the insignia of progress, trash, climbed back into their cart and came down to tell of it and avowed the world would not now be the same.

And it isn't the same. Young people cannot look up and be stirred by the mystery of their own dreams. And I cannot look up without seeing our trash. But we know that the moon isn't a place to plant vegetables and isn't that worth while?

I want to speak of the automobile, and the radio, and the alteration of foods and about Democracy. Quite a lot about that word and its meaning. But first, I must speak strongly about some things relating to the Bible. In so speaking I will be relating to life in general, past and future, and what I will say of these matters will be good. I can vouch for their worth because I've gained from that worth myself. I've been preparing most of my life to write this little book, which I hope might extend to a page for each of my 94 years, though that seems like a lot of pages now. I've done lengthier writing with less trepidation. But the pages to follow will be heavier for their substance is heavy and not written to kill time but to nurture it.

First, about the Bible, for I find the Bible to be the most revealing book of Life ever written.

THE BIBLE AS I READ IT

My first distinct memory referring to the Bible was the little song of : 'Jesus loves me, this I know for the Bible tells me so.' I suppose that's a good reason to prize the Bible; for a little child. There are a lot of people who would like to have such a simple conviction of the Bible's authority.

In my youth there was but little outright questioning of the Bible. So it can only be surmised what the general feelings, and convictions actually were. Much of the conviction was based upon fear, for the constant ranting of hell's fire for the unfaithful was hard to ignore.

If that sort of preaching was your fare from infancy on, then it would be difficult to reject it and substitute whatever contradictory thoughts you may have acquired. It was commonly quoted as a Catholic claim that if you would give your child to them for its first seven years, that child would be with them throughout its life.

I don't know if that was an actual claim of the Catholic church. Perhaps it was an envious reflection of Protestants who wished their own church would show the unquestioning loyalty that was so evident worldwide among the Catholic adherents.

My own quest for basic truth, absolute bedrock unimpeachable truth, entailed Bible reading and relevlant writings, and cautious

1

attendance to churches. But the most active searching dwelled within my own 'self'. A term as large as 'self' is to say 'without end, limitless'. Are we not assured of being created like Them? Created even in the likeness of the Creator.

Faith is stressed, as always it must be with those who want to believe, try to believe, but still long for some sort of absolute which would support faith if it were put to the test that overwhelms so many of our fellow humans worldwide.

I am leading up to direct discussion of certain outstanding matters in the Bible. But since I came into my own conviction by a lifetime of question and search, perhaps you will humor me if I relate somewhat about myself. Who am I to assume any authority on matters that engage the entire lives of countless students? And every one of them trained in language and research that would inundate me?

Briefly, as briefly as one may be when speaking of a lifetime's flow through the consciousness of 'self'.

I have a questioning mind. Sometimes this has been useful and often it is aggravating, for I cannot accept anything as it is advertised to be. When I reached the late teens I fell into such deep depression that I came to see suicide as a most attractive ending for a life so filled with evil, so devoid of the loftiness and purity that youth often searches for and despairs of finding. But at a critical moment I sensed a stern caution against that course which turned me firmly away.

It may have been that same year, probably my eighteenth, that a visionary experience set me on a course that directed me throughout my life.

I give little credence to claims of visions. I think that Satanic forces too frequently direct the minds of those subject to visions. Yet it might be unwise to pitch out all visionary claims for there is as much reason to believe that we are in some degree aided by prayer to God, as that we are directed by Satan.

Just on the face of things doesn't it seem that we are by some means the subject of a creation? As we learn more of the amazing unity of our complex body does it seem at all reasonable that the Creator would quite abandon us to raw uncaring chance, or fate? I go with the conviction that we do have a limited association with our Father, if we want it. That's the rub: if we want it. So, just maybe if a person is adamantly faithful to a usefulness of any sort, just maybe our Father will then give such ones a chore to do. Even a very small chore under God's direction would make a long life worthy of its costs. So, I question visions. And I would recommend that course to anyone else. Unless one experiences an actual vision. Then that's a different matter quite. Do you see how ambiguous an otherwise sound person may be?

Anyhow. I had a wide awake vision in which I was directed, by visual instruction, to stop looking for some worthy career and simply study my own life closely. At the end I would have a modest book worthy of my lifetime.

3

This book in process has been in my consciousness during the past seventy-five years. Until several years ago, I had no idea of what I should write that would be considered of any worth. But as time passed and I viewed its passing, I saw that of all the losses our modern ingeniousness has cost us, the greatest loss has been a demeaning of the Bible.

The Bible has been attacked directly by persons of considerable intelligence and knowledge, so called scientific knowledge. So convincing has this battering been that science has become the bible of many persons. Having made a conscious effort to live close to evident truth, I have never been able to accept any degree of evolution beyond adaptation to circumstance. Surely it is not conceivable that the rules of chance, trial and error, which motivates evolution, can at the same time have the astounding prescience to come by chance upon a cornea of an eye and think, 'well well, this will come in handy if I can find compatible parts, for it is obviously part of an eye'. Every functioning entity requires a plan. Evolution has no plan.

The Bible. I wanted to help other seekers of truth regain faith in that old Book for I had come to see that it was a history of the nature of mankind, which was so far above any other history commonly available, that it belonged in a library elevated and alone. It showed humankind in all our aspects. It treated the good and the bad with equal impartiality. And it is almost funny, in a dreadfully serious way, how those so human humans would run to

God when they had done a lot of wrongs and had run out of luck. They pleaded forgiveness and made rash promises. Repeatedly God forgave them and soon they were right back at worshiping inanimate things of   their own making.

So, I had come into the conviction that there are many of us who would dearly love to believe in the Bible, but it was usually preached as requiring a conversion, a change from no faith to faith. How well I knew that problem.

I had very early reasoned that there had to be a Creator God. Nothing is going to be greater than its creator. That would be simply too unreasonable for anyone trying to be reasonable. So by tracing back the cause and effect, and viewing what I could see of the universe, it was obvious that only God All Mighty, whom we only vaguely could envision, could have created All. That blocked any further thought there. It was much too vast and posed unanswerable things. As my father had remarked, 'dwelling on questions like that can put you in the asylum. When the time comes for us to understand such things, we will understand them.' I find that sound thinking.

But that still did not exclude the need for faith in God and faith in the Bible. I had held my faith in God but never attained faith in the Bible.

When my wife died I needed stronger faith and was ashamed of all the sound reasoning I had used to reject the Bible as being directly of God. So I prayed and from then on had Faith. Just like that. I stopped proving the Bible was inaccurate. It no longer mattered to me that you can't cover the earth with mountain deep water. Didn't God make the earth and water? If he chose to stack it up then it was stacked. I think Jesus made it clear that whatever God willed was done. Zat. No time wait. Who would God wait for? It's ridiculous. Just have faith.

A century ago the validity of the Bible was not so openly questioned. Those who did question it were themselves under question. Atheists, who did not even believe in God. The emphasis was upon gaining faith through conversion; however, I doubt that a good recipe for conversion to faith has ever been devised. Largely it relies upon working up a fever which blankets out countering people. It is known that a portion of those professing conversion do not hold fast. Some are reconverted, although that is not considered a spiritually safe thing to do.

Around that time there was a young law student who was quite rabid about his conviction that Jesus had not even existed. He would argue this subject fervently, and although he became a good lawyer and laid up some wealth, he continued to have this anti-Jesus issue nagging him.

He must have been sincere, for when the time came that he could afford to take a year off he did so, dedicating it to the determination of putting Jesus to rest in a thoroughly legal procedure. He researched everything connected with that period.

But it didn't go well at all. Being a thoroughly honest researcher he kept scrupulous accounts of each historical figure and circumstance and in the end he was amazed that he had a twenty-to-one greater evidence supporting Jesus' validity than he had for any other figure of that time, including the Ceasar.

He gave up law and became a lecturer for the Bible and Jesus. I read his little book but have lost it, together with his name. The reason I bring it up is that when you accept the reality of Jesus, you must reasonably accept his preaching, and one thing that impresses me is that Jesus supports the Bible records without reservations. Jesus, to my mind, is sufficient to prove God's presence in constructing the Bible.

Nonetheless, for determined rejectors of the Book, I knew more visible support would be needed. I was as intent upon finding proof of God's literal presence in establishing the validity of the Bible, as the lawyer had been in disproving Jesus.

I continued searching the early verses of Genesis, for if ever God's presence would be manifest, it would be there. The preachers could rant and fume all they wanted but I needed much more than any man's words of faith to 'legalize' the Bible's account of origins. Proof positive, something you could take in your hands and wring out the living blood of absolute truth.

I had searched enough good writings of Bible commentary to know that what I needed was not being revealed. But I had come to feel strongly that those incredibly condensed verses were as close to being direct communications between God and man as is permitted in this period of our creation. So I said to myself, 'Foster, you feel that these words are essentially as God speaking. You see that each verse is vastly condensed. So read each word as if spoken by God through man. Read now with awe and reverence and watch for meaning'.

I looked down at the open Book. I read the first words slowly, letting them register singly. 'In the beginning.....'

These three words had always served as an introduction to the story that was to follow. Like in simple stories for children that began with 'Once upon a time...' But now, assuming they were the inspired dictate of God, they hit me as a statement demanding a knowledge that only God could have supplied.

'In the beginning' was a statement wholly incredible for any human to utter without knowledge of a creation which began from nothing tangible. It demanded that all which the speaker could see or feel, or even invent, all that had the substance of existence, had once not existed. It had come from no substance whatever, to become rocks and trees and earth. And humans, such as he, had been made out of nothing which then existed. Yet he, the historian, who was made of nothing could think of being nothing even though he could not understand what he was thinking. So he had stated with assurance: 'In the beginning.'

These three words, previously so meaningless, transported me into a conviction that they were written expressly for just such ones as me. These words as I read them, had to have been given to the recorder by God, for God the Creator alone would know that all living matter had come from his own spirit. Jesus had said that his Father was spirit and only he, the Christ, had seen the Father. Without God's instruction those words were imbecilic.

Then why didn't Jesus speak of this particular evidence of the Bible? I don't know. I do know that faith, belief, is not crammed down our throat. God makes it clear that we must move forward by our own free will.

This, in substance, was my response to the opening three words. But how could I be correct? If I was correct it opened a thought which would have been remarked with astonishment by every deep student of this Bible. This Book of guidance and revelation by our God. By our very Father. By the assurance of Jesus, for he assured us that God is his father and our father. We are all members of God's family.

So much came directly from those three words and the thoughts charged by those three words, that they must be thoroughly well known to every Bible student; but known so well that they required no addressing? Like the sun rises each morning without a single notice of it among all the casters of news. So what the words proved must be that I, who presumed to convey some worthy thoughts out of a mere substance of 94 years search, was something of a fool, a hound baying at the moon. Really, an untaught fool performing on a street corner.

I searched again through my commentaries and through several related books, but I searched without interest for I knew what I would find. I would find nothing. If it had been there I would have found it long ago. It was simply in the Bible and too well known for interest.

However, I had a copy of a highly regarded review of the Hebrew religious writings called 'The Kabbalah', reviewed by the French scholar, Adolphe Franck. I had never read it, just glanced through it. It seemed too tedious for my needs. And that's how it was, as I now opened the Kabbalah and turned the pages without expectation and suddenly I was reading my own thoughts. It was precisely the assurance that I searched for.

To read our thoughts in ancient writings is profoundly impressive. That scholar concluded that the uninstructed human mind is incapable of such a thought. My impression exactly. Bless you ancient scholar, and bless you Adolphe Franck, for you made me whole again.

Following those words, which are unequalled by any other effort to join pre-history to the history of the visible universe, we see that 'God created the heavens and the earth'. I had been totally in error about various things that God did, like The Flood. But I still feel safe to trust that the universe was not made in patches but was created as abruptly as anything else that God creates. To our understanding we should realize and bear in mind that God's creations are as Jesus described for us: they are done. God doesn't need to hang around to see that the contractors do it right.

For my own understanding I picture the time that we measure by clock, and by eons, is God's time slowed up enough for us to ride along with it and get a feel of what has been called 'the eternals'. The eternals are apparetly not to be understood. God is teaching us in rank kindergarten fashion, for he our Father is going to do the job thorough and right and that surely will take immeasurable time; eternals.

We have learned to view the track of a bullet by a series of still shots which 'stopped' the bullet. I feel fairly sure that 'time', as we know it, is God's way of letting us see what is not visible to us in its literal state. In order to avoid spending my life contemplating my navel, I assume that everything is in circles. No beginning and no end. Circles within circles and the universe itself...a circle? Within what? Within the eternals? But doesn't that place eternity as a fixed quantity? Shew... The 'space scientists' waste their time and our money on piddling ventures to Mars and wherever. We must be patient. We are not intended to know and understand, but rather to peek and be astounded. Astounded more by our present innocence of knowledge than by what we see when we are permitted to peek. Have patience. Have faith.

In thirty-eight opening words the universe is in tune and the earth is a swirling of gathered waters, or consolidated gas, for the recorders had no term yet for gas, so everything was labeled

11

waters. And now God brought in one of his astoundings and it is of awesome meaning: God said, 'Let there be light.'

I know that things are reeling out but I just must pause here. God said, 'Let there be light.' Like, it's a bit dark in here, turn on the light.

Only in rather recent times have we discovered, or uncovered, the nature of light. A Japanese physicist marvels that the entire universe could be reverted to light. So, light being the substance of everything in creation, it may have been created in coordination. Or it may simply have been there wherever God is, which is to say that it may be of God's spirit or God's will. One thing obvious is that light existed before the sun, because the sun is made of light.

The sun comes in rather late. All sorts of growing things were evidenced before the sun. Maybe it's foolish to concern ourselves with the exact order of creation, for everything of creation comes of God's will. But regarding light, it has special significance in our later times because only now have we found that the universe is created of light. Only now have we found that darkness is also made of light. And this jibes with the statement that God separated the light from the darkness. The plot thickens, but the sure thing is that while the sun gives off a special light or quantity of light, a great amount of growth preceded the sun. Obviously, God can do whatever he wills with light, even to creating darkness of light. If darkness were an absence of light then the universe would die, wipe out every night for there would be no light to maintain it.

For the purpose of proving God's presence in the making of the Bible history, and the accuracy of the Bible account, it seems to me that the fact of light, the apparent discrepancies that must have caused questions to the editors, nonetheless never stopped them from recording it as it is. Or as it was. They could see that it would be more plausible to bring the sun in at the first account, but they didn't. Now we can read the order of things and they become clear. So, who was this apparent contradiction of recording supposed to benefit? Shouldn't this revelation stop those scientists who refute Bible records?

From the first words of the Bible, it is apparent that they never had reason to doubt that they lived on a planet. There is no point in their history which indicates any confusion about the nature of the earth. This is verified by Job, when he reviews some of the marvelous evidences of God, in which he remarks, 'the circle of the earth floating upon nothing'. It was an established knowledge, just as the winds were an established knowledge.

The rest of the world was unable to devise any sound idea of the physical nature of the earth. Even Columbus sailed out against predictions that they would sail off the edge of the earth.

Are facts such as this taught in the public schools? It is not permitted to bring religion into the classrooms. But there seems no hesitation in teaching evolution, which is directly contrary to the Bible. Would it really do harm to tell the first graders that the Hebrew people knew the earth is round and unsupported for thousands of years before the rest of the world knew of this basic truth?

In this country we make claim to living under God. Why, even the ceremony of taking office is centered upon swearing an oath of fidelity with a hand laid upon the Bible. This act is sternly forbidden by God, for we cannot control anything in life, and so we dare not assume constancy by pledging our fidelity upon God's support. We cannot dictate God's support. So, according to the Bible, this nation is led by persons who claim the aid of God yet have no basic knowledge of God.

If we were truly desirous of living by the laws and spirit of God, then we would first have to sweep the entire structure of profit, and control over other lives, and materialism in general, sweep the whole sorry affair out of the door and then demolish the buildings and bury the debris.

If it is the desire of a truth seeker, to find conviction of the Bible's authority under the active direction of God, then surely what my searching reveals is all the conviction one might need. But what I have recorded, and some other material which I will include, should further support the Bible.

However, if a reader has firmly established a rejection of the Bible, then it will take an open mind indeed to reverse the established opinion. For in the homely words of long ago: 'one convinced against one's will is of the same opinion still'. I have found this applies to me and I do try to think and live by whatever apparent truth I can find. Which isn't always an easy thing to find. Most of it gets covered over quickly.

The 27th verse of Genesis might be good to tatoo on the lintel of the doorway to our inner self. 'Let us make man in our likeness'. No matter how we might twist and turn that proposal, it cannot be escaped. It is both a devastating burden if we don't feel up to it; and a lifting strength that can be tapped by each of us no matter how low we may have fallen.

On the one hand, we are advised by Jesus that what God wills is 'done'. And on the other hand is the case of Adam and Eve. The fact is that the Adam and Eve account is being reenacted by us to a degree that must even weary our Father.

It is clear that to become in the nature or likeness of God or Father, and Jesus our Mentor, is not going to be as simple as receiving a diploma. See how abysmally our two ancestors failed. They never got hold of the first requisite, to love our Father, for if we love our Father we love all that is worthy of love. And if we pass on to others the love that our Father gives to us we then obey our Father's will.

I think that might sum the first lesson, the passion to be as They are, for without that complete commitment how could we ever qualify for any furtherance? That was the lesson that Adam and Eve failed. That's why we have this history of failure on earth. That's why we are destroying the earth. And that's what is meant by that terse warning in Revelation, as follows.

Does it seem the Bible is just an old book and not written for continued active guidance? About sixty years after Jesus' death there was a preacher of Jesus' teachings, named John, who was condemned to the Island of Patmos because the Roman powers were bearing down upon Christian preachers. On one afternoon John had a lengthy and complex vision, literally a spiritual visitation from Jesus the Christ. In this book of Revelation, 11:18, is the warning that those who destroy the earth will be destroyed.

At that time it was inconceivable that anyone could destroy the earth. Only now does this warning become valid.

The instructions and warnings of God seem to be almost low key. We might think that God should have belabored his instructions. Since it is apparent that this initial instruction of absolute obedience is vital to the development of Adam and Eve, then might God not have been more firm in his warnings? After all, the promise of being annihilated for disobedience was so immense, then shouldn't Adam have been watched more closely? And being a forgiving Father, might God have not just once at least, extended his forgiveness while this perfect pair 'got their feet on the ground?'

This immensely long period of time that resulted, while we are again given the individual opportunity to respond as did Adam, or respond as did Abraham, reveals the enormity of any disobedience in our growth. Then surely the initial instructions should have been commensurate. And it appears they were not.

However, we now have painfully, terribly, seen the result of our willful disobedience, so we surely have no reason whatever to repeat Adam's failure. We know now that the reward for perfect obedience must be wonderful beyond our conception. And we surely do know too, that we can only be accepted if we approach freely. FREELY! God isn't selling us motor cars in which we must be deceived from every angle possible to overcome our resistence.

God isn't selling us anything. We are as a foolish person to think that we are in a position of influencing God by any ruse of ours. We either see our position clearly, or we again fail, one by one, individually succeed or fail. And we can't complain that we personally are overburdened with temptations. God does not treat us with favoritism, nor give burdens beyond our strength to carry.

Probably we have no way to judge the temptation to do that which is firmly forbidden. Some of us seem driven to criticize the deportment of others, although not seeing our criticism is a strong fault of our own. And it may be no credit to us if we have no desire to criticize. It may be we are so lax in matters of behavior that it's just too much bother to find faults in others. It's a tricky tricky business when we come into criticism of others. I find all the problems I need in criticizing myself.

Like in the matter of sexual desire. I think that a race between sex and automobiles might come out a tie. It looks like either one of them could sink us. I wonder if they are of the one root?

Now just take that matter of Sodom and Gomorrah. God rained down fire upon those two cities because they practiced sodomy. They were gay. Obviously they must have taken it up as a choice for there wouldn't be a city of sexual perversion, as if it were a contagion. But the fact that God destroyed them says that this perversion is no harder to control than any other form of forbidden sexuality.

In this past century we went from rejecting any movie scene showing two persons in a bed, to using active sex as the theme and motivation of the movie. Directors utterly depend on it.

So is God too harsh on us? Can it be that his laws are not reasonable? I can say that on the sexual business it has been a lifelong struggle for me. I recall being aroused by the bare thigh of a large girl when I was three. And a dream of watching sex when I was five. At 94 sex is out of my reach, unfortunately, for it is not out of my desire. And Jesus said one's thought is equal to the act. Thoreau found that one must avoid evil at its beginning. Gandhi regretted that he had never taught his wife to read, having spent their time with sex.

So as the Bible stands it opposes sex for other than its reproductive purpose. It doesn't mention masturbation. At times we need to bear down hard on the fact that the next life has just got to be better than this one. It doesn't matter if we have sex-unlimited or no sex. I trust we will heartily approve whatever it is.

An offshoot of sex is the ritual of circumcision. It began with Abraham. This man was the epitome of unquestioning, unhesitant obedience. When he was near 100 he was directed to have all males in his extended family circumcised. It was a ritual bonding a pact with God. And thereafter every male baby would be circumcised on the eighth day of life.

In quite recent years it has been observed that the infant is not suffiently resistent to the trauma, and beyond the eighth day the awareness of pain increases, causing needless distress. I can vouch for that, since I retain a clear vinette of being circumcised on the kitchen table. I was being restrained by my mother and was protesting vigorously.

I connect the initial instruction, and the recognition of the eighth day in our present age, as a deliberate caution to us in this time of Bible rejection. It may seem too trivial but consider other revelations; the vastness of their reality recorded in a bare few words. I've come to refrain from waiving any pronouncement in that immensely penetrating ancient Book.

There is an incident that might seem unreasonably harsh in the life of Elisha. It was after the elder prophet, Elijah, had ascended to heaven in a whirlwind. At that time the prophet Elisha, who had attended Elijah, inherited the cloak of the elder prophet and was granted the implied authority of this transfer.

Shortly thereafter, Elisha was walking on a road passing a village, and a gang of boys saw him and came out to ridicule him.

19

Now doesn't that reveal an attitude of their parents? It may have been that there was resentment toward Elisha's inheritence of the elder prophets' authority. However, as the boys began to badger God's prophet, jeering: 'Go on up, old baldhead', and repeating this taunt, Elisha turned and faced them, then called down a curse upon them in the name of the Lord. Two she bears came out of the woods and mauled 42 of them.

A little close-knit village and probably all the boys came out to take part in the fun. They didn't have much to entertain them. In reference to Elijah having 'gone up' in the whirlwind, they were showing their cleverness in referring this event to the newly ordained Prophet of God. And the parents weren't watching? And enjoying this affront to authority?

In earlier times, when probably the closeness between God and people was more pronounced, the name of God, in any form, was avoided. The name was too revered to pronounce. They tried to address their God indirectly. Now, the collective youth of the village literally defied God by taunting God's ordained prophet while the parents watched.

On TV, today, it's difficult to find any program above the weather report and the news that isn't profane. God's name serves as as exclamation. I think that illustrates the religious standing common in today's USA.

The violence of that curse upon the boys was a curse upon the parents. It is reflected all the way into today's loose life as exemplified by flappy mouthed TV with its canned laughter every seven seconds. We are so dominated that even our response of laughter is arranged for us. The curse Elisha brought down was mild.

Comparing my memory of early radio, TV, and movies, with the facts of today, illustrates our own downhill progress in morality. Even the word morality is practically out of style.

Another instance of violence, more widely known because of its scope, was when the Jews, who had been led forty years by Moses, were directed to take over a land. They were ordered to destroy the people and the animals. None, not even one infant would be permitted to live. It was as if a plague has existed there and the land was to be scoured.

We are deplorably subject to making snatch decisions upon matters requiring thorough thinking. Our entire disorder of life, the shift from living upon the land, the disuse of walking, unnatural education, profit,- all that has contributed to our present precarious condition was foreseeable by every normal mind, if the mind had been used for thorough thought. And so it is this moment. No matter when that moment arrives.

It's like death. Each of us will die either today or tomorrow. Only a reversal of all that we know of life could make that not true. But how often do we meet someone who is literally prepared for death? The nature of the entire earth's human population would be altered if this simple reality were taught to us when infants and reinforced throughout. It's a fact. Probably no other fact is more pressing; it requires only the thinking, and then obedience to the thought-out conclusion. Not all of us would obey our own conclusion but there would be enough of us obedient to our own revelation that the nature of the world and its inhabitants would be altered. Upward.

Mark Twain wrote a diatribe against the God whom he rejected, using this terrible incident of Bible history to 'prove' that a just and loving God would not commit such an act of slaughter. But he didn't think long enough to realize that the plague of worshiping one's own product of carved wood or chiseled stone would exclude the very source and sustenance and total meaning of life. This rejection of God would have been the subject of Mark Twain's diatribe if he had obeyed observation, then reason, then obedient action.

That wipeout of a small nation presents a lesson to this age as vital to us today as it was when it was ordered by God. During this last century we have doubled back on our own fragile progress and today the result is apparent. But only apparent to us if we break away from our frenetic life and THINK.

You may disagree with me, even to the point of poetically stomping me to oblivion. But still I would have the better of the engagement because I am content with my own conclusion and it is the conclusion of long life, observation, decision, and at least the wish to obey. The desire to obey. Hopefully, joined with the people who are going to win the final goal: True and incorruptible life without death. You just can't beat that. I don't make the error of saying that I shall be accepted into that Life, for I am not able to judge myself to the core. But I sure do yearn to be accepted. At least I think I do.

I believe I mentioned the little warning of destruction to those who destroy the earth. I tend to forget what I have related of the things that I'm set upon relating. The things I've found of most sound meaning in life. And here is one of those beautiful revelations, which I may have related, but if so I resort to the support of an old acquaintance who, relating one of his own gems, would excuse any repetition with the claim that it bears retelling; to which I agree.

It regards the saintly man of long ago who truly lived it. This saint was hoeing his village garden when a neighbor friend passed along. The saint paused to exchange greetings then continued hoeing. The friend watched him thoughtfully as he expressed his thought: 'What would you do right now, if you knew the end time would be tomorrow?' Still hoeing, the saint replied: 'I would hoe my garden.'

I love that scene. I know that I don't need to explain it to you, for you have at once registered your own response, but as long as we are both here and in a receptive mood, please hear my own registered response. That saintly man lived with awareness of death. He didn't suffer from this awareness but responded with being prepared. He thus avoided making wrong choices, consistently making the small right choices which tend to make the day go well and cheerily. He was a comfort to others and a comfort to himself, and this is, I find, requisite to a well worn but well mended life. He was prepared. Packed and ready to depart, for all the goods he wanted to take with him were within him. It went with him now and would go with him when he crossed that faint line.

Part of me would like to be free of all materialism. Like the wonderful dogs who have been my friends. I look at a dog and it doesn't even have a pocket to put its hands into when they get cold. Partly I envy this and partly I don't. I think I could do with almost nothing in a friendly climate, such as I envision in the new life. But I expect even there we will have a few tools. Even the 'saint' had a hoe. The American Indian had little. Very little apparently. And as for a wigwam, it doesn't draw me. I like a solid little house of one good room. One all encompassing room. But I can't get into that here.

Thoreau, in his venture at Waldon Pond, counted 27 or 28 total items inside his cabin. Including pencil and bed clothes and shoes. Everything. Incredible.

See what little is mentioned of human manufacture in the Bible. But what did they need? If we got rid of autos we would cut our needs by seventy-three percent. This percent was by a poll I took on the spot. A sort of one man-on-the-street poll that I whip up on needful occasions and it serves me quite well. I can trust it. It isn't influenced by great enterprises.

In short, as regards the Bible, I feel that what I uncovered in support of its bounderied control by God, had literally never been under cover. I see no sound reason whatever to question the validity and worth of the Bible. Though obviously not a scholar of the Bible or its inferences, I assume the right to read and understand it within my needs. It grows to fit any situation whatever. In early reading of other religions, I found great effort to reach the reality of Creator God and also found that as competitor of the Holy Bible as established by the Hebrew people and reprinted in countless numbers,-I found that none of the other books of religions were worthy of more than a reader's curiosity. I know there are many persons who would kill me for this and feel rewarded. But I don't denounce other bibles for trying to represent a god. I see them failing by lacking the authority which the Hebrew branch retained.

DOWN WITH UP AND UP WITH DOWN

COMMON SENSE

Both tritely and accurately it is said that common sense is uncommon. Yet I go with those who believe that such sense is born into all animal life, and may account for traits in vegetable life in a feeble though persistant manner.

If Darwin had endowed evolution with a joining of common sense, he may have had something with a token of the ability he attributed to his evolution.

It seems that animal behavior insures the blundering action which often produces a predictable response. You step into a stream; you get wet. Then your portion of intelligence decides if the result is desirable or not. If, at least after repeated tests, the animal life records this process along with its decision of a good thing or a bad thing, then a round of common sense is registered. The animal has advanced by common sense. I assume that repetitions applied to other episodes of the animal's life may encourage its overall intelligence.

It appears that advancing degrees of intelligence produce advancing hoards of common sense decisions. And along the way we often see inspiring evidence that even low ability brains may produce surprisingly apt experiences of common sense. We may then be stumped to determine if pure deductive thought is involved. When human minds are involved it becomes more difficult.

My leisurely advance in understanding life has revealed to me that my own mind is slow to draw conclusions from common sense evidence but that it greatly appreciates each win. I do dearly exercise common sense; and suffer humility and irritation whenever I let it slip by unused.

My mind and memory are stubbornly resistant to anything that has been confined by men determined to capture, conquer, label and regulate every little and last thing of life. However, nature will compensate wherever it can, so my mind is unusually retentive of episodes which reveal somewhat the inner workings of mind and somewhat of the spirit. Not an uncommon nature and often at odds with the established aim to gain.

The distinct awareness of the value of common sense came midway through highschool. Prior to this I had been practicing it in discussions with other kids, choosing to support whatever seemed most 'reasonable' rather than what somebody's 'old man' had said, or what 'everybody knows that'. Frequently I would equate myself with the everybody and thus know that everybody didn't know it and everybody didn't believe it. Such discussions caused frictions and no admitted wins but I liked the process of reducing things to their evident base and so I practiced common sense.

The big moment came when our Principle of Schools, a huge and powerful man with a habit of policing the school just by roaming around, sitting in on a class, which caused some discomfiture to the teacher as well as the student. Occasionally he would offer some information which might seem a little off the subject but it would be worth hearing because it would bring something into the present when it had been only a book. He liked to see evidence of a brain working independently.

So one day he ignored schedules and called two classes together in the study hall, along with the teachers. He had a test of a single problem which appealed to him.

'A farmer grew wheat and needed a new silo for storage. The silo would stand thirty feet high and would have an outside diameter of six feet with brick walls eight inches thick. The farmer filled the silo to the top. But a mouse gnawed a little hole at the base of the silo and carried off one hundred grains of wheat each night. How long did it take to empty that silo?'

Boy! I thought: that's crazy. There's no answer to that on two counts. I glanced covertly around the room and everyone had their head tilted to the problem and their paper and pencil in hand and some pencils were actually moving. It bothered me to see that the two teachers, sitting over by the windows, had their pencils really going. I can still see them against the window light. It bothered me because teachers had a habit of knowing more than I knew and some of what they knew was beyond what I ever anticipated knowing. So maybe they saw beyond what I saw. I went through the problem again.

Nope. It isn't workable. I glanced toward the Principal of Schools. I lifted my pencil fingers a half inch. He negatived his head a half inch and I knew I was committed. I waited.

'Time's up. Does anyone have the answer?' I glanced at the teachers. They sat in an air of visible embarrassment. I felt a little sorry for them. It wasn't fair for them to be put on trial like this.

'Foster. Give us the answer.' Like that. Boy...what if?..... I heard the little scoffs of my classmate buddies. Buddies that would eat you if you stepped out ahead and were wrong. If you were right it was the same unless you were an athlete. I was big on non-anything. I said, 'A mouse can't gnaw through eight inches of brick.' It was my best shot. The other was that nobody knew how to measure one hundred grains of wheat. I didn't go for measuring the contents of the silo which is what those teachers may have been doing. Louder scoffs tending toward jeers. 'That's right,' pronounced the Principal of Schools and 280 pounds of authority. The scoffs changed to foot shuffling and I ate it up. The teachers eyes said, 'How come you don't do better in class?'

That experience outvotes at least two-thirds of my highschool bad experience. I had the visible key to common sense. You look for the base of things and build from that. Although I've often used that principle, with some success, I've often failed to use it and gained regret.

I went head-on against common sense by buying twelve new automobiles and ten used ones. I knew better. But I never sat down with common sense and really studied the naked carcass of that automobile industry. I regret that. It is a prominent blotch on my life. It greatly reduced my integrity before my own trust of self. I was sucked in by the system of exploitation. The auto ranks in the front few bloated figures of betrayers of the people. Even betrayers of the self by the self. But isn't that what we all are when we fail to use common sense?

We must go back to somewhere near the earliest history of humanity to find the common sense base which we failed to see, or if we saw it, we failed to obey it.

When we concoct a history of mankind we tend to assume an early resemblance veering toward the ape, both in appearance and intellect.

When we accept the presence of Creator God in the forming of first humankind, we then accept ancestry superior to ourself. I would deny my faith in the Bible by not accepting the whole Bible account. So I assume we were given a good share of common sense. Obviously, Adam and Eve rejected the clear evidence of their Father's perfect rightness. They put self-desires above God's stern instructions, and above the goal of eternal life with Them. That was a rejection of both God's command and a rejection of their own inherent good common sense.

The result of that failure is playing itself out in the soon coming of this world's destruction. If not an immediate demolishment of the planet, then at least a continuation of making it unsustaining to human life. If we can't see that happening then we are on a merry-go-round of fantasy.

At every major point of decision we have chosen wrongly. Using the Bible records as guides, we know that our world was given into the control of Satan, for Satan was what we chose. He lied and we listened to him over God. Can you devise any circumstance where simple common sense was more needed, and could have had greater consequence of benefit?

Well, that probably was the most ignominious flop that we the poeple ever engineered. We have been trying to excell that achievement ever since, and while we have put on enormously more impressive performances, we never equalled that first example because we have never had as much to lose. That little jelly-spined failure in common sense has stopped the clock of progress toward making godlike people of us for some twenty or forty thousands of years. The number of years matters little. The big matter was that we failed at the very start to use that most evident of common sense, and so we set ourselves a pattern which Satan, with our most determined aid, has strained to uphold. And isn't it beyond comprehension that we continue, in this boasted age of 'enlightenment', to go right on giving our everything to uphold our badge and shield of battering good old common sense. It's patriotic. It makes 'sense' to defeat common sense. Our leaders, congress, the big chief, everyone responsible for our treacherous position, with our support, are working overtime to wipe out the world.

But God promised that he would wipe out the traitors. So it behooves us not to support those who demand our support.

The initial failed common sense holds the record. But some of the succeeding are like Cain's example of failing to discover by reasoning, why God approved his brother. Instead of using his mind and some common sense he resorted to murder. It set a precedent that has held up under all manner of effort to eradicate it.

Then, just to take them as they come to mind, there came desire to control one's fellow creature. This was the entrance of profit, greed, cupidity, there are various terms for it but they all mean that one human thinks himself, herself, itself, oneself, worthy of honor and wealth, at the cost of one's fellow creatures. Now, practically every move in life can be tested by common sense. So, if any single human action has earned an examination by common sense it surely must be this filthy stinking practice of using ones fellows to enhance oneself.

Let's test it at its bedrock source. Consider a group of persons, each one of them needing the basics of food, clothing, and shelter. All of these needs can be secured by each person through the medium of labor. Food can be grown to satisfy the need for food. Clothing can be made of animal skins, and if desired, thread can be pulled from certain plants and twisted finely becomes thread which can, by weaving, become rather elegant cloth. Shelter can be constructed of stones or dried clay or timbers. All of these things, and many other useful or pleasant things can be done by each adult, and the children eagerly assist for it is a child's natural pastime.

So, there we have a small community, a tiny community, and each one has a garden and fruits and whatever natural foods indigenous to the land. They share in larger needs. Perhaps dig a fine community well. Dam a little stream to give them a pond to sport in during the summer heat. And so forth.

Did I neglect a need which they cannot perform if they desire? I mean, is there some fine and useful need to have one man of the lot stand aside and direct all this activity and demand a portion of everything for himself which is greater than the portion allotted to the others? I mean, like is one man superior in intellect to the extent that only he can understand the natural procedures of life? A gift straight out of heaven? Perhaps a mark of royalty on his palm? Or can it be that this one man is so incapable of getting his own living that he must be served and granted wealth for his inability? I mean, is there in all the land, regardless of its multitudes, one man so outstandingly grand and noble and smelling of flowers rather than sweat, and with hands too beautiful for labor, is there such a strange creature who is quite incapable of serving himself and his familly as the common people do? If so should it not be the duty of the more favored common people to train this nonproducing creature to do at least some sort of labor useful to the common good? Like carrying water for livestock or some such duty which will be within the reach of such a one?

As strivers, toward the ideal set before us by the Lord, the ideal of equal treatment toward all, doing not to others what you want not done to you; in the vein of this ideal we should give special care to these ones who seem incapable of caring for themselves. Perhaps they were never permitted to care for themselves, like normal children.

Or, just perhaps, they never faced the reality of common sense and thus failed to see themselves as others see them.

Common sense would have prevented the establishing of a city, for only by living upon the plot of land that grows our food, returning all waste to the soil, could the strength of the soil have been maintained. It is so simple to see this. Basic common sense would have prevented cities from ever being conceived. To reduce or remove the means of providing one's own food from the soil marks the absence of common sense. How high a degree of intelligence does it take to deduce that soil grows food and the food feeds oneself and one's family?

How much common sense is required to relate one's hands, fingers and thumb, all swiveled about and directed by one's very own brain, as being suited to the care and use of the marvelous plants growing from the soil? How much further common sense is needed to reason that if this inherent ability and system were interrupted, or made quite impractical by our disuse of common sense, then quite surely this disruption would affect other parts of the life system?

We were granted, individually, this efficient and stable common sense to use toward our intellectual and spiritual growth. Isn't that fully evident? What else would be its purpose? It is the power of reasoning that is based upon the gift of common sense. By using this power, individually, would we in any way desire or support a motor car? For what purpose would we want a motor car?

The auto is a heinous outgrowth of disused common sense. It has provided the soil to grow practically every ailment of civilization. I will need to speak of it separately for it is one of the major trends aimed and quite able to contribute to our destruction as individuals, and so to our destruction as a nation. The process is well on the way.

Do those who use their unearned wealth to encourage us toward destroying ourselves by destroying our enviroment,-do they at any turn resort to common sense?

Is it really common sense to urge we sheep-herded people to borrow and spend at every gulp of industrial indigestion? Is it really common sense, even on a fifth grade level, to judge the condition of our nation by the amount of waste we produce exceeding the amount of waste produced last year, and on back?

Can we lay aside for a few minutes whatever needless distraction we may be enslaved to, lay it down and straighten up and look around and down and up and then center on the One Leader,

Commander and Chief of the moment, and give his performance and intent a fully piercing probe? Can we do this and not be shaken with shame and concern that such persons have gained control over our labor and earnings and the education of our children? Then ask what foreign people we will send our large children to attack, with our own weapons of destruction, that they may thus earn a badge of patriotism for risk of life to a distinctly manipulated cause?

Is it even the most rudimentary common sense to give the use of this insane collection of human destruction into the hands of any mortal, especially one so compacted with self-ness as to believe himself a right director of the massed reservoir of deceived souls which now constitute that which once was the land of the Free and the home of the Brave!

Isn't it quite clear, beyond any power of contradiction, that we are now a people largely herded into non-self-sustaining cities? Quite disconnected from the basics of 'food, clothing, shelter'. Wholly incapable of survival, for two months at the outside estimate, if the umbilical cord of trucks and highways and power plants is interrupted by a very small attack of trained and coordinated men who have been so festered with hatred of our arrogance, and our use of every resource the earth provides, that they choose certain death by active defiance, to life on the dark side of our acclaimed brilliance.

The message and warning was made clear when a couple of bee-hive buildings were bombed by our own symbols of prosperity.

The instant, and repeated response of our Leader was that we would 'smoke em out'. A declaration of the nation's war upon one smoldering enemy, who seems to be yet smoldering and undoubtedly planning. And meanwhile we attack a small nation of oil suppliers who have become a danger to the world and hoarders of mass destruction even rivaling our own hoard of weapons of mass destruction. Except that we know our atomic bombs work while theirs have not been tested nor even discovered. Though they are there, no question, for our leaders assure us so. Ah so. Ah so.

And we are going to prove it no matter how many heroes we have to make in the process, dead or mutilated. We 'will not run from them'. 'We'. Isn't it a comfort to know that 'they' are with us.

Do you think it still has been a wise and beneficial course to reject the safeguard of common sense? God's provision for our advancement?

There is truth which was fully evident at the first of human life on earth, and it has been further proven as research continues. This truth is that each of us, in many ways, is individual. The evidence increases to prove that God created us to be distinctly individual, even while being all of one kind. There is no suggestion that one shall be slave and one shall be master. There is no suggestion that the great majority are consigned to labor toward the wealth of any singular persons whatever.

There is overwhelming evidence, supported soundly by common sense reasoning, that the whole structure of our vaunted American prosperity and superiority of material wealth is precisely OPPOSED TO GOD'S WILL. WE ARE DESTROYING THE EARTH AND OURSELVES.

The entire strength of this nation is organised, by cruelly avaricious men and women, toward the sole passion of gaining ever greater power over the working masses, while causing ever greater disparity of wealth. Never has the cupidity of ambition succeeded upon so great a scale. Never has the power lust been so well served by general circumstances.

The result is that our nation has been drawn into the reverse of any guidance by common sense; little by little, not as obeying a plan, but rather as responding to every facet of life by concerted antithesis to common sense.

Consider this single active trend: The industrialists increasingly have products manufactured abroad at lower costs, thereby reducing their own labor force. In turn there are fewer American buyers of their products. Surely those ill paid foreign workers are never to be customers. Now isn't it apparent that this action will produce a depression of our own economy? And we are not so silly as to think that these industrialists fail to see this, with far more penetration than we see it? So therefore it is a deliberate slowing of our economy that they are producing. When our economy slows critically the value of real property decreases drastically. And the very rich buy up cheaply the holdings of the not very rich. One more step in shifting the nation's wealth into ever fewer hands.

It's a wringing-out process. Just one move in the addictive game of POWER. But have they no concern for the effects upon the herds of workers? Of course they have! What sort of insanity would it be for a dairy farmer to short ration his herd. Even the chicken growers have mercy for their flocks, for if they did not, then the flocks would be less profitable. They have reduced the number of chickens from nine to seven per cage, so now they can stretch their wings, one at a time, and shall we wonder if their meat and eggs are vibrantly healthy? Ah so.

Some claim to have free roaming chickens. Can you see a modern chicken industry with hens laying their eggs all over the terrain? Free roaming? The only free roaming left in this land is the free roaming of words. We need to search under all the plants and trees to find free roaming words that are edible. If anyone is reading my words, they will find them flavored to my own insight, and I can only vouch that to me they taste about right. Sometimes I think them overspiced, but then I give a thought to their objects and I say, 'no, it is not possible to overspice them. Pepper them up just short of blowing themselves up with the hot sauce.' Amen.

And so it is with human worker flocks. The human flocks are started at an early age when their nature vibrates with the command to 'go it, kid! romp and crow and be happy!' and it takes this raw individuality and cages it. Where some of the flock have health which resists caging they drug them.

Conformity is the watchword. And their training from then on will conform to the needs of the MASTERS of industry. They need so many engineers of a given process so the schools crank out engineers. More than enough, in order to keep competition lively and dampen rising wages. A college education is the dream and sacrificial commitment of every unlettered parent for their child. And the result is a more racy motor car and a home with some cultured grass. And they eat with their shirt on.

How did it ever come about? Aren't we the product of the much vaunted 'land of the FREE! Home of the BRAVE!'?

Well, aren't we? Aren't we of the same stock and nature but more prosperous? Aren't we the finest Democracy ever built?

My wife and daughter fear that I come out as viewing life too darkly. I wonder about that false impression as well. For you see, I view life as infinitely glorious. And my inside parts are alive with expectations too wonderful to wisely dwell upon. What I condemn is not life, but I do condemn the bastards of truth who have had life by the neck from the outset, and I am earnestly fearful that they have gained the power to destroy us with blind greed. We are not dealing with humane humans. We are being used as mere pawns in their absolute insanity of greed to take what they did not earn. And by some manipulation of Satan, for it had to be engineered by his superior craft, the common people of this land, whom we should be able to trust, have been steeped in the life-sapping ambition to exceed and excell in every way possible except the gaining of contentment with the least, the littlest, the naturalist, that we are like a great herd of cattle stampeding strait toward a cliff, and we think that what we are doing is alright but must be increased.

I don't know how to get this self-proving truth out clearly except by exposing its wrongs and that does perforce insure a dearth of joy and dancing. But if my words, and the unheard words of a rapidly growing body of others who view reality with apprehension, if we can get our truths out in the open, we will expose the rightful joy and dancing that is being stomped down by the power of wealthy greed that endangers us. I don't enjoy hating, but if I did not hate with all my might toward the damage mounting up then I would not be fit to state that I am a Christian who is supporting the words of Jesus. And I recall how wonderfully he denounced the same tribe that I, and we, now denounce. Jesus was not mousy with his words. He blasted.

This break-and-enter of a foreign land that is now being indulged is but one act which by necessity is revealed. And the guilty ones, hiding behind their assumed authority, for surely it isn't authorized by God, they sit in their safe seats of command and when a misdirected soldier loses an arm or a life they say 'well done oh brave and faithful slave of the right. For you have given your all to protect your people from a dreadful danger.' And the oil, and wealth, and power, will result.

Of course an evil regime is unseated. And he with his entire gang could have been unseated and stomped into the mud at any time those people saw fit to do so. They are a people unlike us for they wrap their convictions in a bundle of explosives and flesh and express themselves thus. And they could have picked off that tyrant any time they strongly desired. Why didn't they? He certainly walked about openly.

Each people is responsible for its own system of rule. And that applies to us. And that is one of the major subjects I will attack. First the support of the Bible, and then the powers which have resulted by rejection of the Bible truths.

DOWN WITH UP AND UP WITH DOWN

HOW DID WE GET HERE AND WHY

First, although much of the early time and the times following may have nostalgic airs and moods about them, I must admit that I have no desire whatever to return to those times of the past. Though much of what has been lost or covered over by life's progress is distinctly better than what much of today presents to us, I still would not go back. Life, by its own term, demands a forward direction. But the wringing, wailing, loss of life, which we have inherited, would be better by measures too heavy to weigh, if we had only obeyed the constant test of Common Sense every day and every minute of the way. In that sense we should review the past. Harp back and when we clearly chose wrong, try to recover the soul of what was rejected and replant it here and now.

That is the mood of what I will recount relating to the past century and the present results.

In the early time of the twentieth century, the century we but lately finished but is not finished with us, we were a rural nation. Not all farmers and farmlets, but some of the good things of rural life were with us richly.

One of the things we lost was the need to walk. Of course it must be evident to everyone, in varying degrees, that nothing is free in this life. A person steeped in his religion may take a strong

45

exception to that statement. God's love is free! We are free to choose right over wrong! And so forth. You can run the gamet of things good and desirable and claim freedom of each, but looking a page deeper you know that nothing is free in this life. And by reasoning from this stand it seems that nothing will be free in the eternal life. There is continual mention of work as related to God and the Christ, Jesus.

It does seem clear, from every view, that work is a part of life which shall never cease. Without constant work of many natures, it might be that we cannot exist. And we would not desire to be free from work. Work of our choice.

Following work of any nature comes the need for rest. Rest is another grace of life, but it must naturally be earned by first performing the period of work. Again, nothing is free.

What we can look forward to in the elevating life is to be able to work, and rest, and live in all our parts and functions, without pain. Yet..even here we must acknowledge a satisfaction from pain that comes from working with healthy energy to our limit. Somehow, it is then a good pain. Wonderful, indeed, are the ways of the Lord. And the Father works each second without loss of one part of a second, or else this universe would come unglued and poof, it would be as if it never had been.

No! No! Never wish for a life without work! Only wish and 'work' toward that time when we will be 'free' to choose what work we want to do. And hopefully, if what I am going to do at any given time, if it requires a tool or two, then hopefully I will be able to find that blasted tool! I have lost a sizable piece of my life hunting for tools. It would seem a simple matter to know where the tools are that you paid a chunk for to own. But it isn't. Of course I know the reason for it. You might think it to be lack of organization, but that is only a part of it. Even disorganized I have a pretty good layout of where the tools are, literally hundreds of tools large and small. But simply too often the tool I'm searching is not there. It is elsewhere. And I lay a goodly portion of that to the 'one' who deserves it. Satan, of course. It's the result of his blanketing the earth with the aura of opposition. Whatever is right will have a nagging, haggling magnetic pull to do what is contrary. It took no more cleverness than it has taken for us to do a multitude of things. Really quite impossible things. Like just living fifty years without being wiped out by an auto in one manner or other. And other things too numerous to mention.

So just the condition of not needing so many tools, and knowing where a tool is, such things as that will give their small worth to making the new life really good. A fine place to work. So, in keeping with this chapter heading: 'How did we get here and why', I should explain that I mean how did our US of A country get into the condition it is undeniably in.

Now you won't get a single agreement with my appraisal, if you are speaking with anyone involved with INDUSTRY. 'Industry is fine. Just fine, thank you.' Industry has got the real people of this USA by the short hairs and it is not going to ever let go until we are a destroyed nation and the INDUSTRIALISTS and the WEALTHY are left swimming without a life jacket.

Do I speak like an anarchist? I was born an anarchist, and did all I could to remain so but the system was too much for me to both make a first rate anarchist because the system had gotten a hold on every last thing but crabgrass. To this day there is not money to be made in raising crabgrass so the system sells stuff to fight it. I say let the dang crabgrass grow and bend down and pet it now and then for it is nearly alone in resisting the ESTABLISHMENT. And boy oh boy, I sure do hate and despise everything devised to make a profit from the labor of a worker person. Of any age or gender or ability. Yes, by dictionary definition I am anarchistic down to and including the marrow in my bones. And if you analyzed my shadow or my aura you would have to marvel 'why this old boy is anarchist right down to and including his shade.' It might not show. I'm not bearded, at this present time, nor swarthy; just a rather harmless old guy, kind of dithering, but don't let it fool you, for anarchists are breeding all around these days, singly and in pockets and some of them publish small periodicals and probably don't class themselves as anarchists. So what is it? I think Bertrand Russell makes a fair description when he describes a certain man as 'he was inclined to anarchism'. A good place to start from. A teething ring for an infant bred into the elevated order of anarchism. Does it seem that I give undo honor to the anarchist? Haven't they been depicted as trouble makers among the gears and belts of Industry? Yes Maam. But they have God's support.

Profit makers, the rich, the greedy, the powerful, are all of one exact pattern, sold by Satan the Great: 'The Leech & Profit System. Guaranteed to gain Wealth, Power and Admiration. Priced at one Soul per the each.' If you make it work you are self-made. God has no hand in it. You even learn to give away a bit of the incredible profits and so be a Philanthropist. God created us anarchists; each respecting all others. We may come upon 'mirror twins', until looking deeper we find differences. And if we look still deeper what other wonders shall we find to chastise our conceit?

In this apparently brilliant age, brilliant by accumulated knowledge over the ages not by basic improvement, we see that we differ not only in finger skin patterns, but apparently in eye patterns. So now we have begun to identify by the eye. So isn't it reasonable that if we get into all the parts of the body that we will find differences abounding? Might it not be that while we remain similar as a species, not at all like a horse, or a dog, even if we humor the evolutionists, we nonetheless may be so astoundingly differing in every part that it would overwhelm the minds of ordinary intelligence? But since the mind of ordinary intelligence and knowledge is permitted to wander quite fantastically without having to prove itself by scientific means, might it not be quite a leisurely expansion of thought to say, 'Well, it looks like maybe God in creating the universe said to the atoms of light, 'there will be no two atoms alike in all the universe.' ' huh? Why not?

The really deep thinkers seem to get into such intricate thought patterns, in trying to understand 'how things happened', without being able to say with childlike simplicity, 'why God made them happen.' Which would be probably the most logical answer we can wisely devise. We do fail to evaluate our situation. I for one, and I am one of a vast many I feel assured, think of God in a familiar sense. The Father to whom we can pray for support, and also the ineffable.....and there we fail to continue. We dare not, and desire not, to question the All of Mightiness of ....God. So we think and say that God may well have made no two exactly similar atoms in the universe.

And so, when we read that we are to be, and literally are now being, created in the likeness of Jesus and the Father, when we read that and trust that, then we are incapable of doubting anything whatever as being outside of God's Power. It is not respectful to go beyond wordless devotion.

Following as closely as my Reverence bids me, I do believe that God made us each to be subject to ourself; and not subject to any other self whatever. We are each a kingdom of matter and will, with a conscience and revelations to guide us. And DAMN the arrogant greed that drives man to profit from the very life of a brother. It is Satanic and is cursed, along with its progenitor!!

That's where we are today. That is why we are on a fast trip to destruction, as a nation, and even as a world. Any people depending upon a continuing line of trucks for its sustenance is an abysmally stupid nation indeed. We have let ourselves be lured like fish to a baited hook. We first of all acted individually stupid, unforgivably stupid, for the course we chose of living in groups removed from direct sustenance. Using our base of common sense, we could not fail to see that when removed from the cycle of planting, eating, returning all waste to the plot of our sustenance, then we set a pattern of earth depletion. That lesson could have been learned within a lifetime. And reproven by every age following. Yet we live in absolute subjection to the will of those who are stripping us of our humanhood. So, what exactly is the strength of our life dedicated toward? To what purpose are we striving? To what are we dedicating our children when we struggle to send them through college? Isn't our life worthy of a grand goal? Infinitely above and beyond any fleeting material success of this life?

We put price tags on the various items for which we labor, and we probably have quite a list of desires. If we achieve one item there will be a next one on the list. And if we chance to win ten or fifty million dollars, won't it quite fill all our desires? Although this is very unlikely to happen, if it should, it would not satisfy our desire. For we cultivate desire itself and so we are enslaved, for desire is never appeased.

If we have barely sufficient for our needs, yet are not suffering for want, and are then not content with our material condition, we shall not be content with millions. Or billions. For there is no satiation to wanting more than is needed. Beyond reasonable needs, including such things as getting our teeth repaired or cataracts removed or a child's teeth really need straightening, beyond such needs there is little, if any gain by having one million dollars or one billion. For that matter, in my case, and the case of quite some others, great wealth is but numbers on a paper.

If the little puppy we now have were in the balance of life or death, and I must choose between his little life or all, yes all, the world's money, I would choose the puppy's life. Why not? I could use a few thousand handily but I have no need for such a terrible burden as a million or upward. Of course I would have to choose the wealth if I could give it where it might do good. Theoretically, it would be a hard decision and I feel sadness at the thought.

If you can understand my position then you know I am not deceiving you nor myself in my utter contempt for wealth. It would be a burden. Like having a load of free gravel dumped in our driveway where we don't need gravel. Wealth is not an item that bears classification. Maybe it's a state of mind.

I do not wish to have power over one person, nor any part of one person. So when I rail against the wealthy, it is not envy. It is that enslaving others for profit or for a sense of power is so despicably loathsome and destructive to others that it stinks in the nostrils of my mind.

But here is a more personal thought. If we desire wealth we are as guilty within our person as if we had this wealth. If we desire to control one or one billion souls beyond our own we are guilty of dictatorship and an enemy of life itself.

It is vital, toward gaining a good life, that we learn to pay heed to the life which now flows through us at this moment. If we don't live in the instant where future meets past, we are then not actually living at all. If we long for a shiny new car, projecting ourself into that future time, then we are not living in the spark of true life which strikes as future flows past, and so we are not living at all. I suspect this applies equally to every wealthy person and to every person desiring wealth.

As I have indicated before, I cannot write this sort of account and file all its parts into categories. I don't even believe this book would be of much worth if it didn't follow the natural course of my memories and thoughts. You can't say to a memory, 'sit down and wait your turn.' If you do you will find the memory has locked its jaws. So I will recall here a memory which I value.

It was long ago on the shore of Palm Beach, Florida. My wife and I were camped inland a mile or so and came to this public beach. I simply would periodically quit my job, rather than ask a leave of absence. I so hated to be subservient to others that I didn't want the thought of returning to employment to hamper my sense of freedom.

It was around midday as we settled on the clean sand. The air was just pleasingly cool and the sun was just pleasingly warm. I worked out a bed on the sand and lay there absorbing the nothingness of life. After some while the body can become part of the nothing and only mental sensation exists. The gentle air, the gentle sun, the pure pleasure of non desire. I thought; is there anything at all that I want? And there was nothing. I thought; 'how long could you be content in this state?' and I answered; 'eternally.' For there is nothing I need nor desire and so I am fulfilled. Nirvana, with the one element which the Hindu thinking failed to supply: perfect elimination of all that distracts you, yes, but also perfect awareness of the bliss that results.

This was a good experience for it showed me how easily God can give us more contentment than we could devise and yet we could live in the creative activity for which we are designed.

That thought has been reached by many individuals but it is still not commonly absorbed, and it should be. We are rich only in proportion to what we do not desire.

It is not so-and-so the Rich one who made his wealth possible. Who is so filled with working strength that he can rightly earn more than double the common wage? And how great a wealth might such a one gain? Proportionately not very great. But only by the actions of many, even hordes of many, can great wealth be gained and therefore great power. So far as my sight can envision there is no honorable way to gain great wealth. Each such one is openly a symbol of Greed to have Power Over One's own kind.

'Oh, but this is not always true,' we might hear. 'This one is motivated by humanitarianism. This one has given enormously to causes which were far beyond the reach of the suffering masses'. Nonsense! All that excessive money was, and is, ours. No one can honorably gain or hold wealth.

All wealth beyond one's vital needs comes of shameless greed! The personal needs of the wealthy and poor is equal. Food, clothing, and shelter still fit the needs of a human. You have but one garment while 'they' have many and each one costing a month of your wage. But can they wear more than one? And if yours is soft to the skin, can theirs' be softer? Or is their skin capable of greater happiness?

When I go to bed, I am tired. And my bed is all that I desire. Of course I am rich in this beyond the richness of most of the world. I assume this is true, although it has not been polled. But I read of those whose bed is by custom a mere plank or two attached to the wall. I wonder if this is by preference; for surely over the years, they could gather something like a soft pad. For me, my mattress is a substantial contributor to the happiness of my life. I sometimes think that 'if I were a rich man,' I would investigate mattresses and simply select the one that feels most suitable. I would do that. I would say; 'how much is this?' and simply pull out my roll of bills and peel them off. So you see, even though my life translates into thrift at all times, still there lingers this passion for a wealth so great that it would elevate me, perhaps above good conscience, to desire the best of mattresses.

Viewed thus, I see that the mattress I have, though quite hammocked, suits the crookedness of my own self, the self I occupy, suits it quite well. I will not say nor think farther on the comfort of a better mattress and think rather how unrightly fortunate I am to own my abode while millions, billions?, do not own an abode all their life long.

As for food, that is a most ill and terminally diseased quantity of our American life. I guess we are thought, by many, to be the best fed, although truly, we are among the most poorly fed. I don't know that I could have survived my 94 years- and counting - except that I early learned of the incompleteness of all our natural foods and have resorted to supplements which I detest. I endure them by the assurance that in the 'new world' which I am hoping fervently to inhabit, the food will once again be food. Not the residue of man's failure to apply common sense to life.

We are, I earnestly believe, in a terminal illness. We, as individuals and therefore as a nation, are dying. Maybe we are dead but not buried. I may be speaking at our funeral services. Not I alone by any means. For while I can only speak honestly as my one voice, yet in a similar vein I am one of many essentially like minded voices. We are not sufficiently nor effectively joined. That shall come. If we live long enough. But it had better be soon.

I wanted to speak about our whereabouts in this terminating span of time granted us by our Father, time to set ourself upon the only upward course open to us if we would continue life. We must, as I see it , reach up, and grab the birthright given to every human being bar none. I speak of the birthright of individuality. It was never given us to treat with such indifference. As if it were no more than a mat to scuff our feet upon. The masses of us without a will to honor, reverence, perhaps even worship, our Right of Individuality. It simply was not ours to be given or bartered away!

We are given, upon our birth, the right of individuality and the power of common sense. We wasted them. Adam, at the first start. Adam again, in failing to instruct and guide Eve who was the late comer. And, except for those who have honored their right, and so kept the spirit of it alive, except for those outstanding ones, we have simply been led and herded into the present condition where our vast cities continue on the forbearance of a few dedicated anti-American Rulershipers. As mentioned, our trucking chain of life can be cut and with it a mass of life which will obviate any hide-and-seek game of hunting down that so trite deception of 'weapons of mass destruction!' Pin the tail on the donkey!

We have made so many wrong moves that we ourselves are at last our own weapon of mass destruction. And we are without elevating goals because we have practiced being led rather than the more demanding fulfillment of being self-leaders.

There is always the viscal memory of our rightful role. It shows up in many small ways, and larger, and quite often in the assurance that it lives by the name of Democracy!

Democracy! In the mouth of government that term is a 'sugar tit' chewed and sucked by the master of leadership and then given to the masses as a symbol of our Democracy. Democracy! How can there ever have been a democracy where the mass voice is never heard?

When the Mayflower met this land, a little boat with not more superstructure than a little barn, from the replica, when the brave and foolhardy people aboard were to venture forth, they recognised a need to join in certain enterprises, and so they agreed to test all joint works by a voice of the majority. Actually, a Democracy. I've not found a record of their minutes, though it may exist, but we need no written record for we are dealing with humanity at any time, back then or right now, and we well know that there always exist those who are hellbent on gaining political mastery. And of course we became so many and widely populated that Democracy became the lie that it presently still is. And it now need not be.

For the first time in the life of any nation we have the near perfect means of establishing ourselves in democracy, and henceforth simply govern ourselves by the majority of our will! It actually can be done. I expect many of us see this clearly and wonder why it isn't happening. Well, it isn't going to happen. We must make it a fact. Not a happening at all. The combining of our determination to be individually voiced in every matter of our concern. Of course it's the Computer of which I speak.

There are things that have developed in the past century which are good, and also bad things. We can take charge of our destiny and either continue choosing a preponderance of bad or strive to self-govern ourselves through the rule of Common Sense, and a continual reference to God's will.

DOWN WITH UP AND UP WITH DOWN

WHAT REALLY HAPPENED IN THE LAST CENTURY?

I will 'make bold' to quickly scan over the prominent bumps in our life as it registers in my experience and maybe it will draw your attention more closely to some very strange happenings.

As I expressed, we were a hand-to-mouth society and pretty much took that for granted. Of course there were always attempts to ease the physical labor but such attempts were small and only directed toward an improved tool to make better use of our muscle power. Electricity had come into use and served for lighting and was feeling its way into replacing the flatiron, which was heated on the stove and had served a long while to so laboriously iron the clothes. But we didn't quickly get into the many uses for small motors.

Even into the 1940s, when I began house building, I did all my work with hand driven tools. The first power tool I bought was a small electric drill. Then I devised a table saw, which I built of wood and had the heavy table top hinged at the rear so I could tilt the table up or down and so regulate the depth of cut. Of course, it meant sliding the work down the tilted top but it did serve. Then about 1950, I invested heavily- one hundred dollars -in a handheld electric saw, and now I have a shop full of equipment. And, do you know, I often look back and see that the old way did have advantages: I didn't have all those ding dong electric cords to aggravate me. Battery driven? Batteries to keep charged and not much power. Some carpenters have gone back to the hand saws and drills and planes. I suspect they even turn out as much or more work except when there is much sawing to be done. Is life really a roller coaster, as has been said?

I got sidetracked there. I must go back again. We were rural. There were cities and slums and we heard of them. Nonetheless, we were primarily rural. During my youth, into the mid-1920s, it was rare to see anyone drive a car to work. We were a village of four-thousand, with various small industries within the village bounds. There was a cloth finishing factory employing 200 and a bicycle works employing about the same, and lesser shops down to such as the shoemaker and tailor self-employed.

The cloth mill produced its own electric power by coal burning furnaces and they used a lot of steam, so they had a steam whistle which was in the charge of the furnace man. He could sound out a flat blast that covered the town, or if a fire was reported, he could carve out a siren followed by a scheduled number of short blasts and everyone in town knew where the fire was located. Saturday noon he did the siren to end the week. That plant also had a five story office tower with six foot high clocks set in its four sides and many people set their life by those clocks. And they had a 180 foot tall chimney which had such a draft that it was said it could draw a coat up and out, if you had a coat to send flying.

I worked in that mill when I escaped school. I had started life with fire in my veins but a twist of fate brought me down until at age seventeen I stood 5'2" x 94 pounds and years of rheumatic fever and Saint Vitus Dance, aptly termed, made life so untenable for me that I vowed to labor myself into mansize and strength or burst my heart trying. And it could have happened.

So against my father's fixed objections, I quit school and went to work in that mill in a loft above the great printing machines. The temperature in the loft was 114 degrees and the work entailed from fast stepping to darting runs directing the cloth coming up over rollers and swings from three printing machines, directing that cloth into carts and ripping off the cloth at a seam and ramming a fresh cart into place. And I tell you, that cloth was loaded with static electricity but you would rather take the shock as you jammed down the cloth than to have it strike the swinging rollers. For if that happened..well, I had not recovered from the St. Vitus and on the rare occasion I failed to control the cloth and it went into 'WINDUP'...

That job was 12 hours a day with 20 minutes off for lunch and only 10 hours on Saturday. It was about as bad a job as any in town, and in some aspects, the best job I ever had. We several boys had a camaraderie that I never again experienced. When conditions are bad, really quite bad, like in front line war, and some jobs like that clothmill job, it can pull a couple or a few servers into as close a brotherhood as they will ever know. It is us, frail us, against the

Monster and we become almost as one. And that seems to swallow up the bad and sweat out a closeness that I suspect will not be equalled short of heaven itself. If that is the universal aura of the next and continuing life, then I guess anything beyond that will be just gravy. All gravy.

Five months of that job, and exercise each night that made the tears roll down, broke the dam that had caged me. And I grew. I reached my prime at age 27, 5'10" x 168 and I was Strong.

That bicycle works made the Liberty Bike, a splendid, light weight tubular framed, no brakes nor overriding gears, no mudguards, just plain muscle to wheel and it was all up to you.

I judge the bicycle as the best of man's effort to move faster than he could run. And, somehow, with less energy expended per mile than in walking or running. Now I have no proof of this, but it simply is true as any biker must know. I suspect in this it is rare in this life. We seem always to lose part of our expenditure to a 'friction' of some sort. But not with the bike. I had an old tintype picture of a group of men, and women, mind you that, posed at the apex of a 'century run.' Fifty miles out and fifty back in the day. The women had long skirts. No mudgards and dirt roads and who can predict a summer shower? And are women not intrepid in more ways than a few? I want to speak earnestly of bikes later.

Early in the century, we had kerosene lamps to read by in the evening. Especially in the colder part of the year. In the summer evening, we usually sat on the porch some while. We were a society of village porch sitters. Apparently, the city people were a society of fire escape and entrance step sitters. People liked to sit out the day's end. Unwind. Relax. Roll and squirm around on the porch floor if you were little. And if riches fell upon you of an evening, it would be in the form of Gramma bringing out a big, a really big, tender 'rusk' with its slightly sweetened sample of heaven and a thin glaze of sugar-water and mysteriously one or two raisins per the each. Living it up. Country style.

Conversation was desultory and low key, preparing for bed, no discussion of world events or any other events, just pre-sleep and you better start for bed or you won't make it.

Later, we would come into radio. We bought the radio, in its earlier form, which didn't work worth a hoot but we stayed with it. We spent relatively large sums for those miserable radios and with such support they did at last get them going and now we went into the home and sat in the semidark and were one with the jokesters or the creaking door mysteries and so forth. Gradually the evening was segmented out in mostly fifteen minute allotments.

Right after supper, we listened to Lowell Thomas relate the news. He was an example of excellence in speech. You felt a comfortable pride in having him speak so directly to you. Then, not too often, yet often enough, he would make some small flub. Nothing worth a pause, but it would draw a little chuckle, nothing more, one trusts, but a little chuckle can require a pretty good chuckle just to wrap it up and of course when it comes to that there is nothing left to do but let out a hearty roar and so clear up the air and be done with it. So he would roar and the announcer had no choice but to join in and we all roared along with the obviously cultivated Mr. Lowell Thomas.

When the second war of the century came, the one that would of necessity finish all wars, Lowell Thomas reported it for us neatly and plainly and we felt that it was a bad thing which was going to require doing and in due course it would be done.

Many years later I was hunting an address on Jupiter Island, Florida, when Lowell Thomas pulled up beside me to assure my direction and we looked into each others' eyes and he thought, 'yes, you know me,' and I thought, 'yes, I do know you and I would like to speak a little with you but I won't.' He was a good man.

In winter we read. We sat in the kitchen. That's where the warm coal burning cook stove sat and where the one 60 watt light bulb hung by its cord from the center of the ceiling. We all sat around and read and sometimes Daddy sat in the oven.

Daddy's back needed warmth. He had been afflicted, beginning moderately at nineteen, with lateral curvature of the spine and it was progressive. The pain in his back and head drove him to use narcotics. One misfortune led to others and his career, which had been so fine, was beaten down. By midage the pain lessened so he was able to crush the drug addiction. By then he was reduced to foreman of the repair shop of the cloth mill where I had worked, just across the river and spanned by the railroad trestle and the footbridge, and the river rushing down below through a rocky stretch.

His back needed warmth on chilled winter nights so he opened the oven door and sat on the shelflike fender. I loved that little old fellow so beaten down but never beaten out. He was in some degree a mother's boy for he was all Gramma had after her husband died in mid-forty. Daddy had humor, and kindness, more kindness to others than to me for he saw in me a wasted mechanical engineer. He was somewhat relieved when I sold a story to Colliers for he respected writers. It impelled him to admit that my life did have some purpose after all. Ah so? He was a mechanical genius at a time when such country geniuses were burgeoning all over the land. Sakes, sakes, what they wouldn't think of next. And they did.

Yes, they sure did think of things. Maybe the thoughts had always been there. That's the way God has laid it out for us. The thoughts are suggested by the environment. Didn't Adam look up at the hawks and eagles soaring blithely around and think, 'boy oh boy, wouldn't that be fun?' Of course he did. He was us but with great health. They looked and wished but there hadn't been all the little parts available to attempt to fly.

Then along came that twenthieth century and the Wright Brothers. So six years before I was born, those stubborn brothers again took their studied contraption to the Carolina beach and one got aboard and they goosed that homemade contraption- which gave a nervous leap into the air and came down a measurable distance forward -and man had flown under mechanical power. Yeah!

Meanwhile other willful fellows were intent upon replacing the horse power and the human leg power with a gasoline engine. Why were they so intent upon doing this thing? The bicycle gave them all the travel aid that made good sense. Where did they intend to go even if they did enginize the horse buggy?

Really, there was utterly no sound reason to make a gasoline driven horse buggy. We walked everywhere within the towns. No problem there. If we needed to visit a larger town, maybe to see a movie or buy a rug, we went by trolley car. They were dandy little cars, some of them quite large. You paid your nickel and climbed aboard and there you were. At ease. No worry about steering, no stink of fumes for they ran off electricity. Electricity which was conducted along a wire above the car, and a little wheel, or 'trolley', on the end of a rod ran along the wire and carried the electric current to the car's motor. So they were called trolley cars.

You were free to look out of the windows or look at your fellow creatures and it was a good little trip. On the way back, an affluent person may have bought a small bag of peanuts to eat while seated in their nickel seat of luxury. I mention the peanuts because I recall, still with envy, the chunky little old fellow who sat on the edge of his seat and cracked his warm roasted peanuts from the little white bag and chewed them and dropped the shells so neatly one after one and Daddy said, 'don't stare, it isn't polite.' So I didn't stare. I just cramped my eyes to be ready if that old fellow might glance up and say 'here, finish them up son.' He didn't. I still wish he had. They were the best peanuts I ever didn't get to eat.

Then there was the railroad. That truly marvelous human achievement. I suspect even God may have approved the railroad. Imagine, all that labor done by human effort. A lot of Chinese as I recall. Today the Chinese make about anything you pick up and look to see who made it. Then, they came over here to build a railroad, and when they got paid they fled, hunted, through the mountains to escape the fellows with rifles who hunted them to kill them for their wages. The Chinese also laundered shirts and the one in our town was fierce looking and asked me things which I could not understand and I feared he would butcher me on the spot. He starched and ironed the detachable shirt collars which men wore for reasons totally unknown and foreign to the neck. 'No ticky, no shirty' the boys would chant as they passed the Chinese laundry shop. I don't know how a foreigner could come into a strange country and act so fierce.

The railroad networked the nation. If you sent to Sears or Wards for a thing too large for the US Mails, it came by rail. Either freight or express, but equally by rail.

Did you ever watch an incredibly long and laden freight train starting up from dead still and powered by one or possibly two coal fired, steam driven, huge drive wheeled engines? Of course you haven't. Nor have I for a very long time. I guess the diesels are ok. In their own way. But they were not steam driven.

You could stand beside that engine and listen to its digestive system and see the escaping steam and then cast your glance back, back, along that line of freight cars and inside of you would come a chuckle and you knew there was just no way that it could be done. That great engine with its great linked drive wheels was very splendid and gritty powerful by itself but hitched to a mountain of dead weight? Nope. No way. And you knew it was going to do it.

For that engine had craft and the red-neckerchiefed engineer sitting up at that little window knew how to excite that craft. He let the steam blast into the cylinder and that engine rammed back into the train of cars. A wrong move? No. The engine knew that it couldn't start that whole mass moving at one time so it jammed a few of those cars together, closing up their links. You could hear them clanking back along the line and so they sat there huddled and compact and poised. Now the engine lunges forward fiercely and it picks up the first car and jerks the slack up on its link so that it has that one car's momentum plus its own. And the second car jerks forward and now there are the engine and two cars and so on, car by car, and you hear the links jerk and so they act as a team with the engine. One by one on down that long line, and then really softly and smoothly the cars slowly pass you by and the engine is on down there and the train is on its way and gaining speed and power and off it goes roaring over the countryside and nothing can stop it. Nothing.

Then there was the matter of the automobile. There was not one sound reason to build an automobile. Not one. I mean not one Sound reason. Man seldom is present when it comes to sound reasoning. There were no roads. Roads were for wagons to rumble over. Bicycles chose their own ways, they only touched the road in two little foot prints and if it came right down to it, you could pick up your twenty-seven pound bike and carry it until it could again carry you.

I've remarked many times and seen it proven: give man two choices, one being sound common sense, the other involved in problems alien to life, and in essentially every case man will choose the way that obviously can never be wholly right. He will choose wrong and them strive nobly and brilliantly to prove that he can make it work. And he may well get it working. But always with bad side effects. I think always, with maybe just a mere touch of good effect. Although that must lay open to proof. I allow that man has made some tools that may be approved by nature. I allow this without full conviction, for nature is so organized that it clearly can produce terrible penalties for any failure to link into nature's pattern. Animals succeed. Man fails because God gave us a choice.

We set trends into action in that twentieth century, and they were very like that freight train getting under way. Each trend is long gone on its own way roaring at great speed, long ago having left the rails and hurtling now through space into this new century and they are aimed and able to destroy us. Their crews have leaped or been flung off and if trends obey any signal it must come from the control Tower of Babel at Washington DC. Little men sit there at their little windows working levers and switches and wetting themselves to direct that which is far and away above their direction for it is far and away above their intelligence. When the cancer of greed for power enters a human system it eats all that may have existed of common sense and replaces it with GREED FOR MORE!

As it stands, it's hopeless. It can't be remedied by any presently available means because the whole Washington Institution is riddled with the disease of Greed for Power. It's expressed in many ways but all of the ways are infected and they have no cure whatever within their system. As always follows wrong choices, we're stricken by evil side effects. The side effects, treated with the same failing cures as the disease proper, shall fail, for it is so destined. God will not let wrong choices result in good. God does not relent for God does not produce, nor dilute, errors.

Man is given freedom, within certain bounds, freedom to select ways in tune with God's evident plan of rightness, which results in advancement toward becoming 'like Them'. Or, in keeping with our right of freedom, we freely choose that which injures in even the slightest way the rightness of God's way, in that choice we direct ourself toward self-destruction. We move ourself outside of the eternity of inexpressible. Oneness with All.

God gave us the means for all kind of physical expression. And if we had the perfect system of health, that we were designed to have, then all of our movements and responses would be expressions that produce a sense of visceral pleasure. Rythmic flow, which we may at times briefly experience in some degree. But never perfect. We cannot know perfection in anything whatever because to do so would reward our wrongness. God does not reward wrong. The very thought is a conflict. So, although I am opposed in general to preaching, I must state that my own relatively long observation and study of life have convinced me that the one goal worthy of our effort must be the goal of following our Father's instructions and trying to understand his purpose for us.

Really, if we learn to be content with the minimum of materialism, and apply our desires toward being acceptable to the next phase of life, the continuance of an advancing life, we then are choosing rightly and all the wealth and adulation of a foolish world will have no meaning for us. Gaining this sense of inward peace, this true indifference toward the racking competitiveness that confronts us in this uncivil civilization, we will even here and now begin to sense what is available to us if we really want it. But we must consciously be our own instructor and encourager and friend. Then we become a friend to others. No need to make overt effort to please. Let our own contentment be the pleasure we give others. I don't believe that following the instruction and example of Jesus should be stressful. Rather, from my experience, the stress in this life is trying to get what we don't need. There is no final goal in that direction. Every day is a disappointment for we never can succeed in satisfying the desire for needless things; there is no saturation level. It is of no importance to be outstanding in some competitiveness we happen to be engaged in. It doesn't matter if our school marks are high or low but rather that we spend time on what is of personal interest to us. It matters not one whit if we do or do not succeed in the sense of worldly success. Shew... have you never seen a corpse? Do you think the great person's corpse is happier than that of his servant's corpse?

Today we are herded into a new 'war'. Actually, the strength and wealth of this so superior nation has shamed us terribly by invading a little nation for reasons which we can only surmise. We can be certain only that we are being lied to at every turn.

We are a nation, a land, rapidly depleting our natural wealth. And each step of the way our choices could have been to our benefit rather than toward our destruction, if we had simply consulted common sense.

The auto answered no need other than the need of certain persons inordinatly driven to command others to do their will. That is a galling sore on humanity which no emollient shall ever relieve. We were essentially rural, even the villagers were supplied with gardens, chickens, fruit trees and time to relax in the evening. We had no need for a machine to transport us to our work or school or church or food markets. Our money was far less disparate from the wealthy and so we were able then, upon common wages, to have better food than we can afford today. And if times were slack, we had our shelves in the basement with plenty of home grown foods in jars. We had chicken that was real chicken, the kind that chased bugs and flapped their wings. We had milk with cream on it and butter that you simply cannot buy today and its flavor is inimitable. Buttermilk was a fact and not a misnomer. Not having ever reveled in churned buttermilk is a tragedy.

And children played games. All sorts of games in all sorts of places and maybe they were clever at them or clumsy but they didn't have parents and coaches urging them to do better at it. What kind of society urges a child to hit a ball and makes it a failure to miss the danged thing? Or Tillie must have her dance lessons? To what end? Dancing is an expression of inner feelings. It has no bearing upon success in life! And where today we are deluged with printed words which are manufactured by persons desperate to meet deadlines and getting out pieces of knowledge which is no way accurate and if so probably doesn't matter a doodly squat. And we had the bicycle.

Now picture this. Here was a society that hadn't been told how little they know and how vital it is to assimilate. And some self serving jerks are sweat-straining to get them into a horse buggy with a gasoline engine to drive it.

There were no roads for the purpose. There was no need to go beyond the next town on the relaxing trolley. If you were busting with energy, you could go like the wind on your bike and feel what real speed, dangerous break neck speed, really is. Or you could sit at home and laugh at the wit and humor of such as 'Three Men in a Boat' by Jerome (K?) Jerome. Or thrill to the latest mystery novel from the local library. Whatever. But the one thing you did not, absolutely did not need, was a gas stinking hard to start horse buggy without a horse to jounce you silly and cost a whole lot of money and move you faster than is safe or conducive to viewing the countryside. You just did not need it. If you gave a few minutes of thought to it, common sense thought, you wouldn't want people to see it sitting in front of your house and have visible proof that you are stupid to buy that stupid thing and you need to be watched.

So they made them, and sold them, and hired great hordes of workers, which required cities built to house them, and an auto to cart them to the work of making the autos.

I too was captive of the auto myth. The false sense of freedom and power and wealth. I had thought myself to be safe from any addiction. But now I see that it was literally just that, an addiction. I see clearly that it was, with me, an attempt to mitigate my bondage to those who had gained power over the workers' very right to life itself. It was a symbol of escape. A drug. It really is, was, and remains an amazing delusion. So senseless.

The auto had but slight reason as a transporter. The bike could have been adapted for light hauling. It could have been made to serve in various forms, and even assisted by arm power as on the railway hand car. I have other evidence to support the bike over the horse buggy, but first it might be well to strip the present auto of its far too costly allure and consider it as a contrivance of transportation.

Before the Wright boys goosed their engine into frantic flight, the heavy emphasis had been upon replacing the horse with little gasoline driven engines. This was not an overnight success. Obviously, the growth of a horse for pulling was a somewhat natural procedure and needed no extensive knowledge nor equipment. And one horse was well known to pull a roughly established load. Depending upon hills and roads and distance and such givens. Without any consultation whatever between the horse faction and the man faction, the horse was serving every need of man and more.

So there had to be at least one prominent reason to even give creative thought to building a non-living creature to pit against the horse. But we were still largely rural, with fuel available to empower the horse. And where was the fuel, let alone the unproven auto which would eat the fuel, to come from and what unproven quantity could be assured? Also, there were all kinds of minor problems to solve.

Like the cost. Daddy had apprenticed at the Liberty Bicycle Works and in ten years, supervised the 200 man shops. And those bikes were so elegantly lean and efficient, and even demandingly affordable. If you earned maybe six dollars or even five dollars a week and saved one dollar a week for ninety weeks, you could own a Liberty light weight bike. And rather obviously, you would cherish that bike. It had been bought on the reverse of the 'buy it now and pay later plus interest' plan that would come into play later with the insatiable itch to make and sell cars. There is a quite different philosophy in the two plans. In the first plan, the buyer holds the power over his decision and action. In the second plan, the buyer has cast away discipline for the lust to have it now and hope for tomorrow even if it does entail higher cost and leave you with a two year old product at the end of the purchase. Meanwhile, you the buyer are somewhat enslaved to the dealer and this does not build strong character and thrift.

So did the average worker of that pre-car possess a stronger character? Great integrity? I think so, perforce. I can't guess about the improvement of spirit, of soul, the you and me that our Father will measure us by, I can't guess if we rack up points in that area. But it is clear that what we do, moment by moment, can affect our attitude and actions. Like an army of young men, fed, I will assume, a diet less weighted by sugar, will perforce have a higher degree of health than the same group left to go their way willy nilly.

So I suspect that our slipping from save-and-buy to buying on a gamble against our ownself, resulted in weaker characters. Characters more malleable to the avarice of those who are dead set upon getting rich, even though it is adamantly apparent that we cannot get rich and at the one time follow Jesus' precept of treating others with the same consideration that we extend to ourself. It's hard to express respect and affection for the one you are foxing out of his share of life's provender.

If we take a few moments to expose the common sense base of our scheming for profit, it proves so openly a choice of right over wrong, that we can just relax and lay back and laugh a bit ruefully and say, 'well, that put's a fix on that.' And we will feel relieved that we don't have to labor at cheating, as we had prepared to do, for cheating always does have a stink about it. Even when we perform it all bathed and clean clad, and bowed in preliminary prayer. Getting the better of the other Guy lowers the status of that other guy so that we are lowered too. For we combat on that lower level which we choose to enter. We just have to get mired if we wrestle in the mire of wrestling away the other fellow's wages of labor.

I can express my own opinion of the so honored profit system by using a bar of Ivory soap as the standard. I would lay the profit system beside the acclaimed purity of the bar of soap, which is 99.9%, and the profit system would excell that soap standard for it is 100% lacking in any degree whatever of concern for one's fellow creature. The profit system was devised and survives upon the practiced knowledge that if you can find a way to get the work-earned wages away from the worker, you prove yourself worthy of your gain and honorable and in line for a monument. Profit is what sustains the frantic search of creating work and products which will demand workers to construct. This will create a sound flow of wealth for you which proves by its own weight that it is superior and honorable. You have created a new need. Bless you.

Without the profit system, every culture we have would mold and rot. Including, I suspect, the institutions of charity in many a case. In ways unseen, just about everything in our life is fueled by profit. Even the preachers of Christ are rewarded by a profit based upon their success in drawing the fallen to their establishment.

If we were a family, including grandparents, and we came to see that these grandparents were kind and thoughtful and knew how to do all the things that needed doing, -wouldn't we grow strongly with love for them? Wouldn't we honor them with our trust? Wouldn't we try to live our life within the bounds that they represent? Wouldn't our concepts of right and wrong come to be as theirs, and as we gained in the wisdom and strength that makes us grow within life and increases our sense of oneness with one another and jointly all with life itself, might it not be said that we are 'growing in their likeness?' So, where is the room for a profit system in this family of mankind? Isn't it good to love one another and to treat all persons as having equal rights? So where is the honored profit system without which the laborers would starve?

There is no room. No room whatever for one person to make a profit from the labor of another. Yet the profit system is a trend which grew immensely in the twentieth century. It had enjoyed popularity among persons of substance from early on. But not until this past century did it really learn to fly. It cannot avoid growing and it can literally destroy our nation of workers, unless we put a stop to it. I must speak of it.

Meanwhile, God offers us the solution and a future far above anything possible on earth now. It might appear to a stranger visiting our planet that we are a mesmerized herd of sub-humans, unable to see that which is right and rewarding, but obedient to liars whose only interest in us is to profit from our labor. Great industries bent only upon using us to bring them profits. It doesn't sound good when it's simply expressed. But it so vividly is their purpose that we seem to find it an unavoidable part of life. As things have come to be in that last century, there is good reason to fear that we literally cannot exist without the profit makers. I suppose if the present system were to stop this instant, we might well literally all die of starvation and bloodshed. And the only good thing to come of it would be that the richest of the rich would perish as well as we. For you see, they depend absolutely on our obedience, as well as we too depend upon the same obedience. Great changes are best carried out slowly and with circumspection ahead of every move. In this manner we can, and actually must, completely alter our present system of life.

Many of us are naturally inclined toward searching for useful thoughts or useful practices and feel well rewarded if we do find something worthy of passing along. That's the extent of my own 'preaching.' I think it is a measure of wanting to communicate things I have found to be true and maybe my experience will serve you too.

Do you know, that twentieth century continues to puzzle me? Even more, it seems, than when I first contemplated this little account of observing and wondering. Such dreadful things we did in that century and must have known what we did.

We had proven by the thousands of wornout farms and tracts of land that you can't sell off the strength of the land and then find some substitute strength to replace it. The real value of that land will never be replaceable because it was too intricate and being the product of eons it cannot be reconstructed in a lifetime. And how often do we hear of any interest of man which concerns itself with the welfare of this world beyond one's own life? And by extension perhaps into the life of one's children?

In my childhood, I began to observe Daddy's interest in our garden. He felt good about the natural things like sun and water and earth. He was a loving gardener. You can often recognise a loving gardener for they will have their hands directly upon the earth and plants. Their tools are hand tools. They will initially get the soil stirred as best they can but their love begins with the planting and from then on tending the plants. Each plant. I wonder if they silently ever name them. Both my wife, Irma, and Daddy were true loving gardeners.

Daddy had a long springy board that he laid down between the rows and he would use it to line up the row and also to sit on. Both he and Gramma would simply sit down on the ground or on the floor with their legs folded back under them, they sat partly upon their folded legs and partly on the floor or ground. It's a joint adaptation. From that close position, they could work around a plant, check its vital signs, leave their aura of affection and slide along to the next several and on.

Daddy bought natural soil enhancers for he knew of the soil depletion. Then we kept chickens and used all their droppings mixed with the dry leaves that I endlessly gathered in the fall. We partitioned our outhouse with burlap so that it was reduced to a one seater with the bulging burlap partition trying to share even that seat. I would drag the leaves in old burlap bags and empty them over the top of the burlap and push them down firmly. Daddy was small and agile. He would climb into the leaf chamber and tromp them down and the leaves aided and abetted him and packed down to half size. I came to hate leaves. But chickens loved them. Each Saturday afternoon in winter, Daddy and I would go into the low roofed coop and scrape out the residue of the week and store it in a barrel toward the spring. We poured the leaves loosely in to about eight inches and opened the little door that connected the upper coop with the underneath area which was spread with ashes for the hens to wallow in. They would come into the freshly furnished leaves, slowly, heads stretched out, darting glances, low sounds of caution and then they would start finding microscopic things to eat. In the week's course they ate most of those leaves. That was village life in the country. We lived on the village fringe.

Vegetables grown then assayed at higher food value; so I read, and choose to believe. The same tests today assay at half the former value. We take supplements. I bagan taking vitamins and minerals, from Sears by mail, when I was about 28 and I've never stopped. I wonder...who really knows...

Why, the experts know, of course. They have degrees in things related. And the fact that they disagree even directly in no way lessens their credibility. Have faith...Ah so.

I'm a sucker for experiment. I would always treat life as a kindergarten even though I were an advanced scholar. And so it is with foods and the eating of them. It's one of the sad trends of the twentieth that we have so depleted and unbalanced our sustaining life-giving soil.

When we hear spoutings of our American superiority, we may wonder if they include or exclude food. For the common sense observable truth is that the most primitive humans are superior in the maintenance of their soil. But I realize that this is not to be compared to open heart surgery and stomping the moon. (that the surgery is as useless as chemotherapy, and the moon shot was precocious children lacking discipline, is nit picking.) Nonetheless, we have increased the downward trend in food values during this past century and it proves deadly. We probably all are half sick. But we have automobiles to replace health.

But how can we not brighten when we consider that all through the ages, from Adam on, we dwelt upon the desirability of flying. Flapping one's arms and moving slowly above the trees. When I was about twenty-eight, I dreamed early one morning that I could back off in the room and with a fast spurt, just glide across the bed and through the open window beside the bed. That this was on the second story was not even considered. In a sense, I was awake as I rolled from bed and backed off for the run. I had never been a sleep walker. I darted forward, dove across the bed, and came to rest with my chin on the window sill. Even then I could not easily reject the dream, for it had been so right. A harmless little gliding about in the fresh morning air. Why not?

Quite a few times I had dreamed that by dint of regulated, hard flaps of my extended arms, I could elevate myself up to tree height, and then as with a breast stroke in water, move along somewhat, but this was not as full flying. Once I had a lofty gliding experience in which I lay prone upon what seemed to be a glider built of select crate wood, and by natural moves of the body, I controlled the flight. However, there was no view from my position so it was essentially a wasted trip, promising more than it could produce.

Quite in keeping with life in the raw. Even the dream couldn't detach from the social art of deception.

But has it no meaning that all my dreams of locomotion are engaged to flight. Why not dreams of fantastic trips by auto? Could it be that the auto is not, in form, included in life's future? Is the dream of flight portentious of that which we will come to realize? My reasoning assures me so. I can reason life quite rid of the auto; 'a work of the devil,' in old times appraisal. And I reiterate, 'a work of the devil indeed.'

But as for flight now, in the past century as it turned out to be? By my own observation and deductions I think that air travel was not a proper choice of endeavor. That we, the 'we' who combined at great cost to launch man and other stuff into high spaces, I cannot see approval of the effort nor of the result. As I may have observed, in the development of the human adult there is no line of demarkation between the child and the adult. Something distinctly adult and wise is granted the infant as its eyes and ears appraise the adults that appear in its orb. Those infant senses are working, and storing, information useful to life in this world. And quite a sum of ungrounded curiosity carries over from infant to adult and if the adult is granted an actively capable mind, that adult may get so deep in its own realm of conviction that what is clearly supported by fantasy becomes supported by jerry built precocious constructions. Like a city in the sky.

Granted that this globe is visibly tending toward becoming outright unfriendly to human life and dragging along with that it is becoming unfriendly to itself. So doesn't that beckon to all constructive and clear minds that we must band together and try our mightiest to set right as best we can all that we have collectively distorted and crippled in our avid grasp for power and the money that falsely buys power? Now just on the face of this proposition, doesn't it ring sound?

Or shall we gather a few choice members, and using the resources supplied by the sheep-mass-laborers, construct a truly clever piece of floating property, a bit of 'self sustaining' property, and with our boat prepared for a sail from earth to the floating city just push off in the dark of night and wave bye bye to the receding globe of earth? Isn't something about like that under way?

To what end? It can't expand, for its materials have dissolved with the earth's end. It can't sustain itself for it is peopled with people who already failed to sustain life when they had everything needful for the job. Are they going to change their nature from concern for themselves at all cost to concern from others at all cost? Human nature needs a certain All Righteous Goal and the elevated spirit and will to hold to that goal without a quiver of doubt. And such ones as this are staying right where they are and centering their ambition to improve the inward human rather than principally his abode. The inner soul deflects all destruction. The abode is what remains after human misuse. God's promise is that the abode of earth will end cataclysmically.

I don't think the earth will end solely because we have misused it. For one thing, the warning in Revelations is that 'those who destroy the earth will be destroyed.' That seems to imply that we destroyers will be stopped. This portent has for some while suggested strongly that our own people are the prime destroyers and will be destroyed while the rest of the world looks on in a turmoil of dismay, for our failure will affect all of the remaining world.

This ending of the world is also foreseen by the science of planet observation. It seems that in its turn, it will burn out. But the Bible goes beyond this and promises a new world.

The wise course surely is to live under the conduct that is directed by the abundant Bible examples and gathered into refined simplicity by Jesus, who gives his earthly life to pay for our heinous fault in our ancestral form of Adam and Eve.

The prominent trends which I observed from early nineteen hundreds and now continuing with a converging force ever stronger, are not quite amenable to neat separation and appraisal. But visibly the gate of moral restraint was flung open by the concerted attack upon the Bible's authority.

There were plenty who desired to have the Bible proven impotent, for there were those same plenty who were restrained only by fear of hell. And there were the ambitious scientists. The strength of conviction given in the few quotes which I found to be most evident, are probably convincing to anyone who wants to believe in God's direct revelations. And if the desire to believe the Book is joined with the desire to obey its precepts, then I think the result will be profoundly reassuring of the continuing life. Not just a continuing life, but an expanding life. And if we dare use the term eternally expanding, we will begin to sense the limitless beauty of life which God has prepared. Just the good company alone will have everlasting appeal. So, without damaging that appeal by any human effort to explain what is not given us to explain, I would only say that no sacrifice of forbidden pleasure will actually be a sacrifice. The trend away from the Bible authority shows up in every wrong move we have made or comtemplate.

The condition of this nation, at present, is a condition of decline. I question that the 'rise and fall of USA America' will ever come into print, for I expect that no nation will escape the End Time. Surely the enterprises of man in this country and throughout the ambitious peoples of the world, are predominantly directed toward goals of materialism. There is no sign of leadership by example of honor, of duty, for the respect of a higher morality.

We are now a nation of evident power, the power of physical force, military force, persuasion by threat. Actually, our directorship, for we have no leadership, stands taller by appearance than it measures by inches. They entered the business of using their various offices at a time when there was money in the till and some credit to boot. Their plans, clearly made to the measure of greed for power, far surpassed the national resources and as for cash on hand, that was chopped up for the first course salad, the fatted calf went down in a gulp and what remains of the herd is rounded up in what will be the last roundup for some time to come. It's been suggested that the directorship publish a book for profit on 'How to lie for fun and profit.' But quite seriously, such a book, written with the embarrassing ineptness of its authors, would have no field of practice for all of that field is bought up with bounderies overlapping. Consult TV to verify that statement. Look down upon our lands swarmed over with indenturing cars which a mere century past had no excuse to be born let alone propagate.

If we can make such progress in ruinous endeavors, can we not make a more modest progress in closing out our manufacture of junk and debt and take over proprietorship of the business?

Is there not a quorum of sane minded, God-inspired Americans to jerk our country out of the corporate hands that now press it to the empty place where hearts were meant to beat? Our first move must be a creation new to this world:

A DEMOCRACY

I wonder if that clutch of Pilgrims, preparing to disembark from the little floating barn named the Mayflower, were driven by shared desires toward independence, or like the little boll weevil were 'just a lookin for a home.' Whatever, and despite their desire for independence, they did recognise that a democracy would best express their possible need for group accord.

It is recorded that before they vacated the ship, they agreed upon self governing by majority; democracy. I don't know how long that agreement lasted. Probably not long. However, the ideal of democracy has lingered on but our nation grew larger as the reality of democracy grew smaller. And it rankles us so that it has become intolerable!

It would not be so insulting if the self-promoting persons in our employ did not harp upon the bald lie that we are a democracy; that we have the finest democracy extant, that we must honor and uphold our precious democracy. Fight and die for it.

Like most all campaining promises, it's a bald headed lie. I don't know why a bald headed lie but it sounds forceful. A damned lie too, as all lies may be damned. Though I would lie without qualms if it was to protect someone from the justice of our system of justice. Did you ever do jury duty?

A democracy of the people has been impossible, or so difficult that it will pass for impossible. Until now. Right now it does appear that we are so capable of joining this nation in true Democracy that the very fact it is not being done, nor apparently contemplated, constitutes a hanging crime. The principals in this failure to provide us a full peoples' democracy calls for the revealed wrath of a public hanging. And shallow burial so the dogs can wreak further vengeance.

How often we think, and hear voiced, the wish that we could somehow know what the people of this nation really do think. Not by a poll! Have you ever been polled by a poll purporting to represent the people? Do you know someone on this purported voice of the people? Do you really believe that when our dominators tell us that we favor shipping our mislead soldiers across the waters to hone in on a deadly enemy of mankind, do you believe that a poll of greater than six joined heads was 'polled?' If so, then bless you for you are not of earth. I do not trust men of government, men in roles of 'public servants.' I want to know what the 'down trodden masses', flashing about in deadly autos, are thinking. If at all. If not, then I want to know about that.

I'm a great believer in letting every last body have an opinion original to one's own life of experience. It is of less importance to me that I might be in agreement with the majority than that I should be privy to what that majority thinks, and if it can be arranged, to get a whiff of why in tarnation they do believe such tripe! Like the advertising lies belched out mouth to tail endlessly urging us to buy buy buy. And, mark this in case it's obscure to you, they are so assured that we have been castrated of all original intelligence, that the prices they quote will be lower by as little as one penny to make the lower number register in the viewers' mind. That is a true revealment of the character of those who provide the materials of life, as well as the materials of death.....perhaps a lingering death.....but death as dead as one may achieve.

So I would like to know what the people, people like us, think. If we had the chance to speak our thought!! Ah...and...ah hah....

Don't you believe that if we really have voice talley, don't you believe that we the people might begin to think? I mean, think about state and national issues. Have you ever watched that TV program where questions are put to an aspirant toward winning a heavy sum of money if the right answer is given? And one aid is the right to poll the audience joint opinion. Then are you not impressed, as I am impressed, by how remarkably, astonishingly often the audience will come up preponderantly with the correct answer? It's humbling. It humbles me like all getout for while my memory for such details is lazy, still I have stored up quite a lot of unnecessary but convenient stuff. I think this little evident fact of audience reaction suggests that we the people may indeed be capable of some quite useful thinking. If we could voice it.

Now! The very apparent source of National Democracy lies in the COMPUTER SYSTEM!! Yes, I know somewhat of its controvertible character, although this is not inherent to its nature. I'm told that 'oh, but the Computer can be rigged.' Ho. Ho. And the present system of voting cannot be rigged? And if the people really get into using the computer for all elections, and for all polling, and for all sorts of joint intelligence of this general nature, then I think we would find ways to make the computer at least more honorable than the bash exposed in Florida not long past. And also, do you suppose that Florida stands alone in such a swill of vote tallying?

Whatever.

Look. Those computer people are very clever in their field. It is strongly reasonable that they could, on some slack weekend, devise a little 'Voterbox', as a temporary label, a little box equipped simply to register messages on a small screen, and to have a yes-or-no touch register for any current issue whatever. Anything. Local or national. A little Voterbox which would verify any person of the household who has been registered with the Box. Verifying each member, by perhaps finger scanning, or eye scanning. It seems that we are so universally varied that I doubt this would be a limiting problem. And the actual voting would be concealed by the structure of the box, so that coercion within the family would be prevented.

I am fervently encouraged by this apparent opportunity to at last make real the long suffering desire for a Democracy of this people. I have not the slightest doubt that ancient graves of patriots would rumble and crack open upon inauguration of a Voterbox to sit in judgement upon every issue affecting 'we the people.' WE THE PEOPLE!!! Amen. Oh yes! Amen!

I have spent some considerable thought on this Voterbox idea, which surely has been slumbering restlessly in many a mind. And I believe that if we swiftly recognise and honor this opportunity to join America by common majority voice, through the Computer systems, we then will have established a new pivoting point in our history. We will have to push it!

There will be instant and powerful opposition to any effort toward bringing 'we the people' literally into expressing determinations in such an uncontrovertible fashion. A voiced opinion which cannot be falsified by that so sweet little clutch of opinion-tayloring exploiters of humanity lodging in the Tower of Babel, Washington DC. They will stomp on it with all their well heeled custom-built shoes. For the fact is that such a system would be the shroud of the false leaderships we have been increasingly forced to support with our very life.

If there is any doubt about the strangling noose around our neck, try to raise a family in FREEDOM! Try to buy and own a little plot of land and build with your hands, even of the clay and rock and timber of your own bought and paid for land, - and then escape the notice of a little weasel who will arrive to assess the value and determine the tax you shall be obliged to pay to those who hide behind the snickers of 'public servants.' Did you ever, in this so advanced age, attend the sale of properties from the courthouse steps, properties going going gone!! To satisfy the tax necessary to uphold the system of public servants which 'we the people' had no voice in establishing?

From the lowest to the most lucratively honored (self honored) positions, our government is the rule of intimidation by an official 'MOB.'

A small group of armed, lawless, ruthless preditors can control a much larger, and latently a much stronger, social territory. Most of us want peace, but are too timid to bristle and battle toward gaining and keeping that peace. We have to reach the point of explosion before we set to right the wrongs which always are apparent.

To have a majority rule at all times, operating with small cost, available to every qualified voting citizen, is so unveiled a threat to the whole shambles of our falsely called 'democracy,' that they who would instantly suffer from a true democracy will turn against it with all their usurped power.

Nonetheless, and 'notwithstanding', there is still enough red blood in the veins of this automobile addicted social order to say to their keepers and herders, 'ENOUGH! DAMN IT AND DAMN YOU! BEGONE!!'

And it would be done. A new age of human freedom would be seeded and watered at that instant. It can be done. If it isn't, we may as well cross our arms and be measured for a coffin of our choice. For this nation is being exploited by a system of falseness which would turn our stomach if it were stripped publicly to its naked obscenity.

Is this the ranting of mediocrity? If great issues cannot be tested by common reasoning, then the issues cannot be great. For, whether we will it or not, we are every one of us created children of God. And if we accept that primal evidence of God's presence in the Bible, then do we not see that God wants each of us to know basic rights and basic wrongs? So, that which cannot stand upon the unadorned rock of common sense, cannot stand.

Please consider the several following conditions:

We are said to hold elections which reveal the will of the people. We are given two or several candidates from whom to choose. How did they get on the ballot? Probably it would be as representative of our will, as it would be to choose the contents between two closed hands. How much will the office pay and how much did it cost? It's phoney, but deadly serious in result. It's gangsterism.

People!

Thousands of years ago, we were told how we must live in this world of our God, our Father. But we were given the choice to listen to our Creator and recognize that only our Creator could advise us rightly, or to not listen, to try various things and thoughts right from the start, even though we actually have had the brain power to choose our Father's way. We are not latently so damned stupid that we couldn't see that God's way was at least Common Sense. It's a sorry ass jerk of a sub-human intellect that can't see we would all gain if each of us honored all others even as we would be honored!

That's all we have needed to do and still is all that God wants us to do.

Instantly our whole life would change. We no longer would try to get the better of others. There would be no profiting. No rich and no poor. We each would consider all others and so we would be considered by all others. Do we need more? Do we want more? Do we deserve more?

Let's quit our stupid mucking around and start NOW to live like humans and not like mad dogs. LET'S OBEY OUR FATHER WHO MADE US!

And if an official fails us too badly, shouldn't we be able to swiftly take a plebiscite on whether we should serve him two weeks notice? If a people cannot discharge their employee then it's a farce, and we had better have it revealed. Ah so!

Our system would be greatly improved and representative if we used the Voterbox, open to every voter. If we want to cast our vote for Uncle Joe who needs a job, it might seem a foolish vote, but not quite. Uncle Joe would be pleased.

And, I may have mentioned this: the swearing in with hand on the Bible. Even if the holder of the Bible is a well known preacher, that swearing is strictly forbidden by God. This makes both the preacher and the swearer false.

And we are taxed. We have no real representation yet we are taxed to uphold whatever those in power determine. It seems to be the privilege of the president. Isn't that presumptuous for an officer who was only intended to be the chief of those whose duty is to carry out the will of the elected representatives? What nation of persons with a vestige of good sense would elect a great batch of rule makers and purveyors of funds and then install one person to determine the taxes. Also, just as a bit of news with the morning's coffee, - we may learn of the bombing of some unheard of site, even an almost unheard of country, with the population of a big city but scary as all get out and we better bomb them. As one higher-upper remarked: 'Why have all this military might, if you don't use it?'

At times there are too many autos built. That's a glutted market. This is dreadfully serious. It doesn't mean that we've caught up with our work and can have a holiday. We are so closely dependant upon each day's pay. So the all wise president displays his forceful leadership by urging the people to spend any money that has been overlooked by the taxers, and buy something. A new car would be a token of patriotism. It would also bring one more older car under the compacter. You want new cars at the top end and compact cars at the bottom. You have to keep this roundelay of make and waste to be prosperous. Thrift and save for a rainy day is now hogwash.

The 'health of our economy for the year' is gauged by the amount of new things bought against the amount of new things bought a year ago. And junked of course. Thrift is our enemy. Waste and buy is our creed. So to encourage this, manufacturers effect 'improvements.'

Now the reasoning behind this national policy insures that we have a progressive society, leader of the world, provable by the size of our military with its weapons of mass destruction. The common sense behind it may be elusive. Most things that don't exist can be tantalizingly elusive. And we have our share of them.

First, if we try to disengage ourself from all we see and hear around us, and turn ourself inward for a brief discussion with whatever is left of our common sense, we will look out upon this country and we might well think: 'the solid materials which comprise this land, and the environment surrounding us, may be finite. We may run out of them. Maybe not us, although there are strong signs of that happening. Quite strong signs when you get at the truth for it is already happening.

It started way back when we shot all but thirty of those huge buffalo that migrated like great rivers. Shot the bastards clean to death. Great sport. English sporting gentlemen came over in both envy and brotherhood to ride the trains that went out to shoot the varmints. Shot them for meat, the poorer chaps did. Shot them for trophies, the sports chaps did. Commoners shot them for hide, then when it glutted the market, they shot them for the tongue. But the pure sports chaps shot them for the hell of it. You only live once, so live it up. You shoot a buffalo and then walk up to it. Its size. The bulk of it. And you walk away a bigger man for it. Yes indeed.

But we have matured. We raise some of those near extinct buffalo. It's too late to recover any of the carrier pigeons. They migrated like clouds to darken the sun and roosted nights so thick on the branches that men, grown up men, and boys, went out evenings and clubbed them down. Filled ditches with them, so they claimed, but men will brag about things that make them real men. Real things. Rolling a cigarette with one hand while riding a horse and such as that. Owning an automobile that has got something like three, four, hunert horse power under the hood. 'Man...you gotta feel it.'

And that's good? It's the way to please your public servants. Like your president who says get out and buy stuff and boost up the economy. I wonder why they call it economy. Doesn't economy mean something else?

There is no limit in greed. Greed is self perpetuating and it does not permit a surfeit. The whole thrill and purpose of life would end for the greed infected ones if there was an end to greed. Use up everybody's oil but save ours for last because we may need it if we don't find another avenue of wealth to capture.

But what about the obvious plan of God? The Creator God? 'Well didn't he claim to make nature and aint nature the greatest waster? Look around you at the leaves and water and fish spawning and lightning fires and everything? It's waste up to your gills!'

Nature never wasted an atom. Everything has a planned use. Only man wastes. We burn oil which maybe wasn't meant for burning at all. But we sicken the air and the air sickens us. That's what always happens when we contradict the common sense of nature. We don't get away with a single infraction. We look away and go on with our petulant greed and waste.

Nature burns forests and makes smoke that can kill you. Yes, especially if you mess with its plan of frequent burnings by lightning of undergrowth so the fires will be low and soon green over. The smoke is ash which falls as fertilizer. The opposite of pollution.

So our government favors such things as cars and trucks and roads and jobs. Slathers of jobs to make stuff to sell and make profit. Just why is it good to have lots of jobs? We should live without any jobs away from home jobs, jobs for the direct provision of food, clothing, and shelter. But that wouldn't make profit for the rich. And that is an ugly fact.

If we had avoided that system of promoting jobs to grind out profit, it would have preserved our entire natural wealth. We would not have robbed one little snot nosed kid now facing a deep dark future. I pity them.

Our government, by my sight and reckoning, draws and builds persons who don't have any hankering to go out and labor. They use the tax flow, the river of golden dreams, and they do things that help their team and help reelection and try to hide the truth from the populace. Like they hid the truth way back in the early time of Social Security when we the commoners supposed we had, - was it five or ten billion dollars in the fund? A billion was a whole lot of money then. It had been used without any accounting. Isn't that amazing? It was all gone. Our governing protectors had divied it up for state's projects or new shoes, what does it matter, it was stolen. Group theft with each conspirator supporting the all. No, I don't trust government. And if a person hangs around with them, no matter the wide-eyed innocence that brought him into the pack, if he hangs around he will come to smell the same as the rest of them smell. Bad.

But really, wouldn't you think that they would get just too damned bored with gaming for more chips of greedy power? Wouldn't you think a massive combine of maybe three of them would break out in hives of suppressed honesty and blow up the whole works?

Isn't it in the realm of slumbering humanity that we the people would waken one morning, I mean really waken all the way up and say, in stentorian voice, or vibrant female dulcet tone, whatever, waken and fill our lungs and blast out: 'what in firey hell are we doing to this once upon a time grand land with our senseless, utterly stupid drive to make more and more money even though the rich are going to get it, for it is so written that 'the rich get richer and poor get lice!!!'

Wouldn't you think so? I mean when you look it in the eye, don't you see that if it is good to have more and more jobs then you are going to have less and less time to live your own interpretation of life? Am I wrong? If so, put it down in clear writing for it will need heavy pondering.

Or can it be that we are not taught sufficiently about the need of having time to visit the human soul living in there? Are we afraid of the questions our soul may ask of us? Like, why have you spent these years striving to excell your brethen or sistren, to put them down so that you can get more of whatever it is all the rage to get..? Striving to get your kids into a 'better' school than they need, and study something that they may have no desire to actually know, and to eat and drink of that artificial life, until a treacherous 'retirement' time comes. Retirement from what? Do you ever ask yourself just what you want to retire from? If it's so stressful or boring that you have had a smoldering hatred for it, all this large hole in your life, then might it not have been better for you to do else? Better for you and your soul, sitting there in a rocking chair looking out of a small window upon what I presume is the real world, and wishing that you and the wife and the kids would come in and spend some time with visiting. Get to actually know one another.

Don't you sense the air of that spirit in early morning when the little shop shutters of life begin to open and you try to catch the aroma in a cup of fresh brewed coffee? Of course it never can be quite brewed as the air of it promises. All of this sort of thing which you have been trained, 'educated', into excluding from your life, for sensitive spiritual stuff is not the stuff that executives are made of. Not the stuff of fortunesk. Not the stuff of RECOGNITION!

Have you never?

No? Too bad. Too bad. There's so much that begins with the rejection of what is called 'material success'. We hear of 'the measure of success'. But I feel suspicious of any success which can be measured, for this calls for camparisons and none of us can accurately measure the relativity of individual development. Individual success.

Success in one's general character used to be important. I recall one modest success which rested upon common sense. Since it combined training of character by common sense, it remains in my mind.

Smoking. I tested that one Sunday afternoon when I was fifteen and several of us boys were walking along a wooded stream. I bought a cigarette from the older, seventeen year old boy who had left school to work and could now enjoy the freedom of smoking. Probably not because he liked to pull smoke into his lungs instead of clean woodland air. Air was then apparently clean. He had his reasons for smoking, that is why he smoked. I suspect defiance was a major with him for it was a noticeable trait.

While I knew by observation and information that smoking 'cut your wind', and I knew that I had no excess of wind to encourage cutting any of it, I don't think that this alone would have kept me apart from cigarettes. So, I gave this smoking boy one cent for one cigarette. This netted him a modest profit for cigarettes were going at twenty for fifteen cents. He was suspicious about my assurance that he gained in the transaction, which may give a clue to his mathematical acumen. So I lighted it. He didn't charge for the match. He hadn't been charged for it. Fortunately.

I state openly now, for I've grown above some common levels of shame, that I expected to experience some manner of sexual stimulation from the cigarette. Without inquiry, I had assumed that the probable enticement to draw a man into the cigarette habit would be linked to sex. The billboards had been slowly bringing a lovely female into the thing of smoking, so this fed my conviction that sex lurked in there somewhere. The lovely female had advanced to the bold stage of holding the cigarette, sort of handing it to him, and if that didn't reek of sex then we boys didn't know what sex did reek of. I think one lovely female was lighting the thing as it hung from the too-handsome seducer's face and we boys looked at it and said 'if she smokes, she will go all the way'. We were cheated by her for we had quite loved such a lovely female just out of a protective sense. As for the seducer, we would have smashed his face in. His kind were not good to have hanging around. We had one such fellow in town who would fit that billboard. We had seen him on a Saturday evening standing on the street waiting for the trolley. And he wore a suit which was strangly suited to that kind of fellow and a soft gray fedora hat and his smooth face had patches of white talcum on it and you could see that he wanted it to be in patches to show off his tanned pink cheeks and believe it or not he was leaning on a cane and we knew he was not lame. He wore one gray suade glove on his right hand, but the glove for his left hand was draped over the curve of the cane. His bare hand kept the arrangement together. We looked at him closely as we walked by and you would swear he came out of a magazine. Which, of course, he did.

We were just boys but not every one of us was still pure. We knew things about life. And now, as I purchased the cigarette from this older boy, I could see he had some tentative patches of talcum on his tanned and pinkish cheeks.

I smoked that cigarette down to the hilt and there was no sensation in any degree sex rousing. Maybe one cig didn't do it. Again the transaction and down to the hilt. Nothing. A treacherous deception. A lesson stored with others that combine to suggest that you do well to trust business men only as far as you could throw them. But I tend to be thorough. Three cigs and three cents would cinch it.

So I did it and then I took stock. This was common sense in action. My mouth and nose had been used for a chimney and they tasted like it and smelled like it. My hand stank. I had wasted three cents. But I had gained. I would never need to carry that little pack of cigs in my shirt pocket, and the matches, and be uneasy and nervous if they ran out. I would not have to earn that fifteen cents per pack, per day. Not ever. Grandmother had taught me well to always consider an expenditure by the times you would renew it.

It was easy to see that smoking would cost me over fifty dollars a year, five hundred in ten years, and in thirty, it would be fifteen hundred plus compounding interest which is hard to figure. But it would mean that a man could buy a little house through the local Building and Loan and own it outright before he would be too old to work. And if you wanted to do the double house deal you could be paying off your house with the tenant's rent and even do another complete transaction. Boy oh boy....there was a lot to think about, and a lot of people, for various reasons, do not desire to think.

I don't believe that having a national voting system, a system on demand as it would be, would turn this nation into a mass of deep thinkers. But is that a reason to deprive people of the opportunity to express a thought?

There are those who strongly desire to 'be their own boss', and they are willing to work toward that end. And there are others, probably the greater portion, who are more content to perform labors which don't require any effort or risk beyond assigned work. I think this is understandable and probably necessary to our general society. But does that mean that one person should prosper financially at the expense of others?

Perhaps I expect more in a trend to protect our individuality than is possible in actual practice. But my philosphy is guided more by the direction one pursues, than by whether a goal is reached.

In keeping with the practice of common sense, I refer broad matters to simple, symbolic expressions. And so I quite often recall that pleasing episode of the saintly man hoeing his garden. I know I have spoken of this, probably twice before, but some things not only bear repeating, but benefit us by their repetition.

If this nation did in fact, in practice, uphold a system of general order which would require not leaders but persons seasoned in the ways of living a kind and useful life, persons well aged in proof of their rightness, then perhaps we the people might live essentially as did that wise saint. For as it is, we don't have a distant and beckoning goal. We do live literally a machine to mouth existence. And if an adventurer in new products could come up with a little machine which would masticate our food and supply all the digestive enzymes in proper portions, and then just squirt that puree through a tube held in the mouth and reservoired from a little plastic nicely fitting appliance laying over the shoulder or hung from the neck, then don't you see that we could circumvent all our problems of not having time for chewing, or of having ill performing teeth, or having no teeth whatever, even as I,....is there a need to elaborate farther? We assume it would be artificially natural flavored to taste good. And we assume that one could perform other occupations meanwhile. Or just recline idly or listen to some jerk kneed sound vaguely related to a long passed ancestor of music. A quick movie. Driving at rocket speed in our horse power extending in our vision out beyond a hundred yards. Oh, it would be wonderful all around. Every step of it approved by nutritional authority. Truly a machine of person feeding. And aren't we edging toward it? All the prepared stuff put up in cans and the people with their little containers of liquids with a convenient plastic straw teet right there in the mouth. Not machine to mouth existence? A movement in that direction? Quite.

I think that everything we can do to gain or regain the establishment of individuality of our obviously individual selves is a good thing to pursue. I think individuality should be pursued and approved from childhood by each of us who feel its rightness. I don't agree with overt persuasion except where one infringes upon the rights of others. I believe that we can best be persuasive by letting our convictions be known. Like the saint hoeing. He didn't preach it; he lived it. And both then and this long while later, he affects me by having expressed the way that I too approve.

Do you know,-Jesus was not a crusader. He performed miracles, yes, but he didn't emphasise them. They were not his message of rightness and salvation. He lived in God's Truth. In this, Jesus was adament. Less persuasive than informative. If you had the lock on your heart that his words fit, then your heart was opened. But it was by your will and effort that his words proved themselves in your heart.

God made us absolutely individual. I have no doubt, and there is not room even for surprise, that God has not made two alike of anything. He surely didn't have to. And there is no sign in nature that proves he did. It can appear that he did, and still not be true. In any event, God did make us singular. Does that leave any least crack to enter into another person's life and sap out that person's labor for our own accumulation?

I read me back and I question: 'Foster, aren't you too condemning in your pronouncements against such ones as control our lives? Should you be so vehement, and even repetitious? Isn't there a mark of envy there? And are you enough above those whom you condemn to permit your judgement?'

I don't know. I'm assured that I create resentment and hatred toward me; assuming that persons do read what I am now writing, or feel it is worth the reading. But I must be honest or I would be better silent. I have no way in which I can reveal the intensity of distaste for anyone who profits upon another soul of our Father's personal creation. That each one is held in life by our Father's direct will is firmly expressed by Jesus when he states that the Father is aware of a sparrow's fall.

It simply is not approved that we use another person to our advantage. It is mean and low and offensive in every facet of offensiveness. It is what I would condemn in this little book, subsidiary only to the proof of God in the Bible. If I had the ability to make my condemnation stronger, I would use that ability. To see those individuals accumulate money which equates with human lives, reduces them to something lower than subhuman. I might look at them and wonder if they truly are thinking beings.

Democracy is a move in the right direction. We don't have a choice of whether we should pursue it vigorously; the question waiting is when will we do it. God, our Father, never left an opening for debating his instructions. He offered us the way toward perfectness of Life. Life of His Creation. Then he left us to individually choose the Right, or to choose the wrong. He gave us the opening toward Happiness. Might we desire more than happiness? Is there something missing in happiness? But it was happiness contingent upon our choice of listening to our Father, and we knew He was our Father; or of listening to the incredible smallness of vanity. We dropped down to the level of that vain angel, Satan. The same angel who so craved stardom that he offered Jesus his power over us, which we gave him by listening to him rather than to God. He offered all this if Jesus would honor him just once. Jesus contemtuously refused.

If Jesus had accepted, he then could have rid the world of its evil. Rid us of all pain and sorrow and at the same time destroy our chance of redemption. For, while our Father could grant us absolution from our sin and make us perfect, he would be removing our power of freedom, and without freedom, we are no longer fully alive. We could never go on and become in the likeness of our Father and of Jesus. Jesus saved us by his sacrifice, which confuses me.

How can it be that we are ruled by men who profess faith in God, may pray each morning for guidance, and then live a life dedicated to gaining and using power over their own kind? Literally over their own brothers and sisters.

But it is a fact that such men exist and a fact that very likely the huge majority of we Americans would love to be in the place of these grossly rich grossly powerful persons. Apparently the truth also is that none of these aspiring individuals, whether poor or rich, have a conscious goal of being acceptable toward the next life in which we shall be judged by our Father to determine if we are fit to continue life. This present existence is not the life God offered us. It is the test period given us in which we can prove ourself for acceptance as aspirant toward a continuance or toward death. Success as measured by money or power is worse than merely worthless. It is self-destructive and insultingly injurious to one's own people.

We might draw apart from our present activity for a short spell, like just sit down with ourself and put aside all the vanity of thinking ourself needful of money and power and fame and whatever we find attractive of that nature, just draw apart and look at this life broadly. Scan along this life from birth through all the stages of growth and whatever achievement we have gained, or whatever achievement we have wanted to gain, for in this scanning of our life we are viewing our soul, and it matters not to our soul if we achieved worldly position. If we scan life in this cursory manner, we shall come quickly to death. To the end of this preliminary experience. Need I go on from that point? We end stripped of all we own. Even of our clothing, naked to the soul. There we stand before God. And mind you now, bear down on this reality: nothing of this world is with us. No money, no power, no honor, nothing. Then shall we be at peace, as the saint with his hoe was at peace? Or shall we too late pray in hopelessness for the acceptance which we did not earn?

I fervently hope that I've passed over the baseless things of this world. I can say without a shade of doubt that I would rather live and die by the code that Jesus gave us, than to be granted all the highest honors that man has devised, even to outright owning the world on a lollypop stick. Clearly, all wealth beyond our simple needs is Satan's invention, with our admiration.

POSSIBLE RESULTS OF DEMOCRACY

We know that those in power are earnest in their desire to have us believe we actually are a Democracy, even though it is wide open truth that we are, from beginning to end, only the chessmen which they use against one another as they seek to win win win.

They will fight with anger, fear, and hate, to prevent us from having a People's Democracy. But assuming that we use our greater power, we will in fact achieve a full democracy.

Then what in the world are we going to do with it? Everything is so well filled and authorized by authorities which we've never met and never will meet. We will often feel alone and uncertain standing outside their impregable fortress. For they own everything. Maybe they even own each other. Why not?

The probabiltiy is that we will effect very little change at the outset. And I expect it will need to come slowly, as the great freight train starting up, just as all other trends of the twentieth century.

That twentieth century broke down the slow advancement of civil gains. It struck at the heart of such gains, for it attacked the Bible upon which this nation was essentially founded. With the Bible discredited, the people's unexpressed desires became the flag of freedom. We did march under it, and we still do. For our nation has no standard to hold higher than the desire for this life's material success. Goals and desires which end with death. The whole life given to no lasting goal whatever. How can we fail to see?

We should publicly discuss the Bible, then whatever can withstand the battering of opposition should become part of our common knowledge. Surely, the few parts of the Bible which I have quoted are far more real and provable than the accepted claim that the oil reservoirs are of the remains of dinasours.

Have you ever seen a trace of crude oil gathered under a dead animal? How deep must the carcasses have been to have made a reservoir of anything faintly suggesting great reservoirs of oil?

If a scattering of literate people in the country boldly examine and so support the self-evident truths of the Bible history, we might then slowly regain a national goal toward which we could raise our site and our trust. And that would be salubrious.

With a Voterbox we might bring persons of our own choosing into positions of 'Administration'! Not the misnomer of 'public servant'. The will of the democracy needs to be administered; so it is not a serving, it is simply administering what has been determined by vote, for the present, with no assurance that it will fit any prior or future dictum.

In general, we probably would continue the present system of public office, however, all along the way we would be selecting the members of administration by our popular vote. We would choose at the local level those whom we know and most trust to represent us up to the next level and so with the gaining of experience they would be able to choose the next assembly. But, by arrangement, we would be able to oust any person we deemed to be better replaced. By such degrees, yet quite rapidly, we would gain a working association with our own chosen government.

As for competitive party systems, is this not surely a sophmoric sport? We don't need a contest of wills for power and spoils. We simply need administrators who will mature in their work as we mature in our experience.

Should we have a president? When our Congress of States representatives come to a conculsion it is then necessary to put the decision into effect. That should be the job of the executive office. It should not be the job of one man to determine if the peoples' representatives should be obeyed or rejected.

Even if the bill in question is unwise, the Congress should be responsible for the bill. Good or bad, one man should not be allowed to contradict the congress for that is not democratic.

We should have an administrative office of perhaps three or five or so, with a research team to answer any such needs for both the congress and the administrators. But that office should be administrative. They should be able to question or advise but with no authority. Not capable of starting a big fire by setting fire to the sofa. At present we have essentially a one man rule, or we have a one man hindrance.

Truman was right when he said we need but one party and that would be the Democratic. At the time I thought he was making a little joke of frustration, but I see now that his closeness with the scene made his statement quite wise indeed.

Roosevelt had tried to form a sort of national democracy. A government for the people. His plan for a flat social security with all money held in bond and ready to ease recessions was altered to its damage.

TAXES are ever an issue for discussion. There is a simple cure but it's a medicine too bitter for those who need it.

The cure is to make a simple bar-graph of incomes, ranging from the least to the greatest. Then we the people would make a reasonable attempt to determine just how much we really need for a given period, and by sliding a horizontal gauge down that bar-chart, talleying the accumulating sums, the exact taxes would be determined. You then take a razor sharp blade, administer adequate seditives and whacko! There's the money for the upcoming term. Next year you repeat this. Soon you will be lopping halfway across the graph and that probably will suffice.

But there is a further need regarding money and its associates. It has been ventured in failing experiments and has been called Socialism. While the idea is humanitarian, it never could have worked well or long because the temptation is far too great for mortal man to resist such an opportuntity to get POWER over the process and that was that. History books have hashed it and it needed hashing.

But with a Democracy such as here contemplated? And add to this a new system of Money.

From my readings and queries I gather a strong suspicion that 'we the people', the 'working stiffs', and very possibly the professors who profess a higher knowledge, and have a higher knowledge, in some things, I suspect that among us the ones who have a clear understanding of what one billion dollars actually is, are indeed rare. One billion dollars is not an easy number to grasp because it doesn't deal in familiar items. One loaf of bread, or one SUV auto, ring the cash register, visually. One billion dollars does not.

I believe we need to understand one billion dollars. Clearly those who govern and herd us do not and care not. After all, they don't earn their living loading garbage trucks or shingling a steep roof in a threatening wind, and have one week's pay come up short before the next one is earned.

Grandmother owned her home, lived in two rooms converted to an apartment, which she 'housecleaned' every Friday, and Daddy inherited the house and had six percent interest on his savings of thirty-two thousand dollars. They did okay.

And we're confronted with a society in which there are living, walking, billionairs. My uncle was a thrifty country doctor and ended worth one-hundred thousand. He was 'well to do'.

Here's a billion:

Save one hundred thousand dollars a year, which is a tidy sum to save, and in ten thousand years you will be a billionaire. But if this is correct, how can a person become a billionaire? We must be more realistic. We hear of corporation high ups coming out with a year's tip of a million or more. So if such a one tucked away one million a year, how would he fare? My little calculator insists he would need to hang in for a thousand years! Mental arithmetic supports the calculator.

Shewww...... A million dollars isn't really much money these days. What has happened over my lifetime? So far as I can tell, I'm alive and well. Not strong like I was. I used to deadlift 300 lbs 15 times for my back and now I use 80 lbs and it is heavier. But as for apparent health, I feel healthier. Happier. More peaceful. Kinder. Although I don't sound so in this writing. And twenty years ago, when I quit working for wages, I earned my top money of five dollars per hour. What has gone wrong?

Well, without really knowing, I know that what went wrong is greed and deception. I hang it on greed and deception. And I am quite convinced that we need a new kind of money. A money built upon equality among the human race. Not this fat dog over here getting meat and bones by the wheelbarrow load and these skinny hounds impouned over here getting the smell of it.

It's our life we are spending! Is a day of your life more to be respected than a day of mine? Or the reverse? I'll fight you over that; for it involves the justice of our Father!

So, this little research introduces the need for a new form of money. A money composed of 'fair exchange'. A money impervious to fluctuating values. Isn't a loaf of bread, made of identical materials, a loaf of bread in any age and quite unaffected by the price number on its wrapper? Does the food value change with its climb during my lifetime from ten cents per loaf to two dollars? It's laughable. And deplorable.

DOWN WITH UP AND UP WITH DOWN

MONEY

Of course the need for chits, or some sort of accounting notes, naturally came along with barter. Certain persons came into situations or were driven by desires to sort of specialize in a commodity. Maybe one chap liked to make some kind of shoe. Another chap found hunting suited him. But he needed shoes and the shoemaker needed hides so it was a simple swap. However, the hunter can only wear one pair of shoes, with a pair in reserve. So the shoemaker gives the hunter a chit for additional shoes equal to hides received and the hunter goes on his way. Until he needs corn. You get tired of only meat. Corn is easy to dry and carry in a little leather sack like the Scottish sheep herders, and probably numbers of others than Scots. So the hunter barters a shoe chit for corn and the corn chap either goes to collect his shoes or trades into some other field of common need. You can see that this could get to be a pretty handy little arrangement and also can get so out of hand that it is a mess.

In came government. Could you keep it out if there is money to be gained? And with adjustments here and there you've got a floating currency going. But you need something solid to back currency, not hides and corn. So the government decides to make notes backed by gold.

Now, let's use the old common sense test and see if gold really is the backing agent. If it is, then there will be a bad imbalance. But what makes gold so valuable anyhow? It does lend some worth in maybe filling teeth and plating harder metals and making electric contacts, but those things can't be the value makers. How about labor?

What is a greater constant, governable by mankind, than plain old Labor? LABOR! Is there a nation on earth so poor that it has no labor? Then why not go to the root of money and base it on labor?

AN ECONOMY BASED UPON LABOR

What I am driving toward is far above its individual parts. I am proposing, in awkward steps which can be joined by good will into an impervious globe, I am proposing the following system.

Heretofore we were handicapped by lack of full and immediate communication. That was in the years BC, before computers. Now we have the computer, and it is threatened by the swill of money makers to be degraded just as TV, and everything else that can be converted to profits, is degraded. However, there are quite a good many of us concerned for the soul of our country. We would like to see America grow into maturity. We are really tired of seeing a common adulation lathered upon less than needless forms of diversion. The taste for excellence must be formed early or the taste for the vile and stupid will fill the young minds and this is evident today in a measure to cause concern. This nation could not do better than to set its site on a realization, activation, of the Golden Rule and like giddy aspirations.

I don't mean that we should expect to achieve such fineness. I may be foolish, even by choice, but I am not a fool. I believe in individual striving toward that shining light of Rightness. And I see that a nation, like drops of water making the seas, is a great pool of individuals and every individual who plants their feet and pulls toward that shining light is pulling the whole nation toward that shining light.

Again. For it is so important. It is not what we have been, or done, that will judge us- it is what we are doing NOW that will determine our worth and our future.

So, floating on that aspiration, I propose that we adopt a currency based upon labor. One day of labor shall equal an adequate income. Or one hour of labor is ten units per hour? It's a good working number. Now everyone working an hour earns ten units.

Yes, there are complications. But they aren't entirely unpleasant. First, as I see it, we take a heavy blade such as was once used to whack off heads and we whack off the head of Profit. There. No more profit. No more big salaries. Just the one level of income per week.

We must keep in mind that a great reversal can only be fairly achieved by cautious degrees. Revolutions are desperate and futile. With a full communication among the people we could gradually eliminate numbers of industries. If profits were cut by taxation until real demand of the people halted it in any given enterprise, then by a natural alteration in habits we could reduce overall labor needs to perhaps three days a week. All weekly income to be equal. The disparity in the nature and attraction of any given employment would self-regulate the hours of work that would be required to receive the week's earnings. I think what I propose necessitates the ownership of many or most businesses by the workers.

Pleasant jobs would require a full week. Like maybe twenty hours. But dangerous or disagreeable jobs might require much less time. I think there might be openings for a person to work more than the basic job, if money were needed beyond the standard week. But always the labor would be controlled so that everyone, regardless of ability, would have work at a liveable wage.

There should not be any inheritance. No opportunity should ever again be permitted for growing a fortune. There might be large employers but no one would be paid above the standard.

Questions rise and they would require thoughtful solutions. Has there ever been a time, even brief, when questions did not rise? If we regard our present system, or customs, and try to envision bringing them into a new world and new society we would be daunted by the thought.

The great thing is to eliminate profiting. It is too indecent to countenance. We must have full employment. Everyone must have a living wage. Full health care is a given. I must express some opinion on education but for now it must be fully available throughout life. There is not time to begin and end the gaining of knowledge.

If we would make all our floating money, our bills of exchange, valued on the base of labor, there would be no deflation nor inflation. The idea is not compatible. If we made this work it would draw the rest of the world into a like system which would provide for fair trade.

We should reclaim some things of the past, things which we should have retained. It is in our nature to go too far in whatever we undertake. Whatever direction we choose, whether it is in the direction of greater and more, or in the reverse direction of smaller and less, we will probably overdo it. We seem to have difficulty in getting our machine rolling and then we have difficulty in braking it to a halt. We are a far from perfect people and by some activity of Satan, with our assistance, whatever direction we have moved in, we have found that the money makers anticipated us.

We should have kept the railroads and gradually rebuilt them on a lighter scale. Between 68% and perhaps 93% of all long distance trucking should be carried on the rails. Of course as we progress, the fine wisdom I anticipate will grow out of our new democracy, so we will come to see that a conservative 73% of all the freight that trundles over our highways should never have been birthed. If all profit above slim working capital is confiscated by tax, there will then be little incentive to continue needless manufacture; and less yet in starting upon unrequested enterprise.

The auto, with all its attendant cities and roads and wholesale waste and deception was, and continues to be, a most heinous error. If we were determined to have the auto at all then it should have followed Buckminster Fuller's 'Dymaxion' which he developed to the stage of manufacture in 1933 and was then thwarted by the established moguls of automotive deception. They, the whole tribe who were in that trade of prostitution, they were scared out of their panties when they saw what one intelligent and thoroughly honest inventor could do. Fuller had used the common sense approach of going back to the beginning. Everyone driving an auto chariot should be just once passed on a mountain curve by that Dymaxion, as were my wife and I. Just once, see that simplified perfection of wheels sweep smoothly and quietly by and be gone from sight, and know that in every way but size and cost and ineficienty, that Dymaxion was clearly superior. If that design had then been adopted there would be, among a multitude of other gains, there would be no misdirected boys and men messing around in a little country across the waters, hunting for masses of potential danger and incidentally safeguarding our oil. Everyone killed in that childish grab is a sacrifice to the arrogance of a small group of ambitious wealthy manipulators with ambition toward gaining ever more wealth. Why? Oh, why? Little unfeeling boys waxed large and strong in greed, money, and power. Boys who never have become men. And we let them control us? That makes us as guilty as they!

With democracy firmly in place, we will be able to see the rightness of reverting our money system to labor-backed bills of exchange. I recall when President Roosevelt decreed that all gold-backed bills were to be exchanged for bills literally backed by promise of our government to pay, and we were given a time limit to trundle our bills to the bank. There undoubtedly were some quite miffed persons but they did what was decreed. It didn't phase us young fellows. We were wiped out from the stock market fiasco and hadn't one gold backed bill among us. But the point is that it was done. And just as easily our whole money system could today be exchanged for labor backed bills.

Now, really, wouldn't that be a fine and uplifting thing to do? Why mercy me, we herded people can say 'let's just do that fine and uplifting thing and then perhaps we will move toward being full human beings, created in God's image, and no longer answer to the commands of our herders' voice.' Yes, we have the power to do that. Why not? Who is actually running every particle of our so-called economy right now? Do we need the herders? We need them to make out our payroll? Not if we pay ourselves with labor backed bills. Not if we the people control our own government. Not if we remove the profit system.

Not if we accept the offer of our Creator Father and become wholly individaul, each of us a unique person. Not perfect. Not often even good looking, if we look at ourself critically. But the inner person, the human thinking and aspiring soul, the singular marvelous we; we who are actually attached to our Father as long as our soul lives. Who else is keeping us alive, even after death? Our magnificent president and magnificent congress? Let's stand up a little straighter even if it hurts our back, and take hold of our brief destiny here on earth. Let us LIVE, and DIE, in FREEDOM!

Caution. Even all fired up free people need to move with good common sense, for if we do use common sense and caution, and concern for one another, we are absolutely assured of success.

EDUCATION

Education is important. Otherwise we are less than a worm or a beetle, for the Lord has given them all the education for which they have need. But as animals advance in brain power, just so do they advance in need of education.

So we need to be educated. But with that recognition the whole business of education explodes. Our purpose on this earth is to give us individually the opportunity to be accepted into continuance of life under the instruction and glorification of our Father. And I suspect under the instruction and guidance of the Son, Jesus, who did give his life as the sacrifice for our so foolish sins. I think that our Father created the entire universe to be in the care of the Son. That seems to be right and beautifully right. For obviously we are not likely to be able to 'see' or communicate with the Father, as we will be with the Son as the human manifestation of the Father.

If you, of your own conviction, believe that there is some other purpose in life here on earth, then I do urge you to think hard on that conviction and see if it provides any satisfying reason for our existence! And the awareness that we exist! Are you more eager to be mislead by all the deceptions that Satan and his Powers are now permitted to use against us, deceiving us into believing that we may do all we choose to do even though we are told strongly to refrain? Told by the Bible which is provably God's instruction, if you, or I, obey these urges, then let us inquire just what good are they doing us and just what harm shall they do us. Pondering a question like that can make the short hairs on the back of the neck come to stiff attention.

An occasional lucid glimpse of what we are paying for that which has nothing worthy to offer us, can make us suddenly very wise and quite brilliant persons indeed. We may find ourself making a fervent prayer for forgiveness.

And that sort of thinking is, to the conviction of many of us, the root and fruit of education. An education expressly and fully directed toward becoming as acceptable as we are capable of becoming. Acceptable to Jesus and our Father. Never with a thought of becoming acceptable to crowd or peer judgement. Let us be acceptable to our conscience and be quite indifferent to any other acceptance whatever. If we obey our conscience we won't do anything to unjustly injure or offend anyone else. And what more can we do?

There are many people today who do not like the public school system. But we are involved with just getting a living and meeting the damned bills and worrying about the failing car and other stuff which we should not be nearly so concerned with. We are so involved with all the matters which in themselves are not worthy of worry, that we have no time to meet the natural needs of educating our children. Nor of educating ourselves.

If we will get hold of our entire system of life in this shaky nation we will distinctly have far more time to do the things that are natural to life. We may find ourselves actually engaged in educating our children without planning to.

We are all aware of how kids will nag us to 'let me do that', 'I can do that'. And how often at that time, we are in a hurry and we brush their request impatiently away. There is a five year old girl child who lives close by and visits us at any hour from seven to seven and she can be a mite aggravating. And also more than a mite interesting.

We are rural people. I personally think everyone should be rural, but how can you be employed in industry and finance and all that crap and drivel and still be rural? Well, to avoid any attempt to answer that I will speak of this child Annie. She likes to sweep with a full-sized broom. Just picture sweeping with a broom that is twice your height. But she is determined. Maybe we are sweeping off the little concrete area at the back door. I manage to get some good licks, which she sweeps into the dust pan I hold. She sweeps with some absence of control but even in this short trial I see that she is trying to find the best motion. She is being educated. She is learning about what is part of our life. Sweeping.

Then I need to bring in a large wheelborrow of split wood to fire our woodburning home heater. We recently put in gas as a backup, but we burn wood. Lots of it. Now this raises educational thoughts and opportunities. First, the child wants to push the empty wheelborrow up to the woodshed. I say, 'it is too heavy for you'. She weighs about twenty pounds of energy and probably twelve pounds of bone and lean muscle. 'No, it's not too heavy. Let me try'. I catch myself. I recall wanting to do everything my father did. I wanted to open the can of evaporated milk. He impatiently handed me the can and the opener to pierce the lid. I was three. We were sitting at the noonday meal. I pushed mightily on the opener. I faced public failure and sensed my puniness. I got down on the floor and pounded on the end of the opener. It hurt. It did not pierce the lid. I 'prayed' for my father to relieve me from this so embarrassing labor of failure. Then he did. 'So you couldn't open it?' But he did offer the suggestion of humorous compassion. He was a compassionate man but harried by pain and troubles. He had not been a good teacher in this incident. He was putting me in my place.

I remembered all this in a sweep of recall and said, 'Well, you can try it.' I knew she couldn't push the wheelbarrow because it is a big one, deep, with handmade handles much too thick for her grip. Even too thick for mine. The path up to the woodshed starts there at the backdoor on a bit of level wood walk. She got her hands under the handles one way and then the opposite way and her thin arms were spread wide and golly but she got that thing up and moving. Immediately she confronted the curving incline on the rough path and double golly but she kept that monstrous barrow going, up, over the fresh dirt of a waterpipe trench, across the yard and right up to the woodshed. I had no medal for her. I said, 'You did good. I didn't think you possibly could do that.' She wore the medal with quiet pride. She was five, she was attending school, and she was liking it and was learning things and had no orders to sit, stand, sing, and if you display real health, flowing-over energy, then we have no choice but to drug you. We can not permit children of abundant health to sit in our United States of America classrooms. It is simply too disruptive. And I agree.

I agree in the powerful sense that classrooms are too unfit for a healthy child to enter, let alone be inducted. Such schools as we have, nationally, are preparatory to providing fully regimented young adults who will do just what they are told to do so that they may come under employ in a capacity needful to the manufacture of an automobile or dishwasher or bathroom fixture, or any of the probably thousands, and could it be millions of fully crappy and partial crappy money extracting enterprises which are the result of greed in the marketplace.

And underlying it all is greed in the heart, and mind, and soul of our brethren keepers. For we can't escape it, - these persons of monster-minded greed for power, and the wealth which measures power, they are of our own family. And we, as a society, are so warped and knot-holed and termite ridden with the decay of our humanity, our vibrant and loving humanity, that we must not only acknowledge our siblingship but we have been so mind-warped by our own lust for wealth that we actually admire our masters. What percentage of us are truly not envious and desirous of wealth in abundance?

After so great a length of time in which wealth and envy of wealth, desire to win, to beat down the weaker ones and step up on their shamed faces toward positions of higher station, after so great a length of time, -forty thousand years?- and the chief advocator of humaneness for humanity having been nailed to a pole and raised up as an object of shame, after all that time and the vastness of desire, greed, being the water of our life, how can we ever remove ourselves from what we have built?

Shall we say, 'well, there have always been some who resisted, so why cannot we all change enmasse as a society?

I agree with that desire to make beneficial changes on a national scale, but I believe we must approach our problems from the very close company of our-self. Obviously what has gone before is gone, not recallable. And what is to come is not yet consequent to our will. But what we will, and what we strive for at this razor edge of transition from past into future, at this timeless transition, here lies our full life, our whole life and all the wealth of living which we acquire. This 'now' time is our test. This is our whole battlefield of life, this instant of a noninstant, and we are free to fight and win or not fight and lose. If we fight to win, that is to win over our own faults, we shall not lose. No matter the outcome.

Toward this awareness and appreciation and the will to rule over our own non-instant of life, constantly, and with as much contentment and good digestion as our surroundings permit, aiming toward the full value of this awareness, is the object of education. What else could it be? It is eternity, this nonplace in which we live and which conveys us in obedience to the orders of our will.

In this sense we cannot fail to teach and be taught. It is life. Our children, along with us, should live in this full school of life as patently the only place worthy of life.

If we live right, and our children live and work with us, we will achieve the basics of wise education with a joyful goal waiting for us at the end.

There is so much to be taught. All that pertains to the matters of corporeal life. Let the children grow with us as we grow. If there is work needful to attaining a living, and the growing child is attracted to that work, let the learning of it come by apprenticing and experiencing if at all possible.

Work, of one's desire, which requires a college or university of training, should be open to everyone. Child, adult, what does age matter if the will is to learn? We should revert to the earlier halls of lecture. It matters not one whit if a person fulfills a formal test of knowledge. Let that be proven when the need arises. No child, no person, should be 'graded'. No student should be required to study that which does not appeal. We are individuals!

I favor all primary schooling to be 'hands on' wherever possible. Then study in small groups where discipline is not needed, for only those desiring the learning will attend.

The great majority of knowledge needful to life can be gained by this means of growing up into it, and furthered by study of books.

The goal is always vital to this life. The conviction that life is endless, else it has no real meaning. For all that ends is then nonexistent and equal to having never been. If memory of us shall remain in those yet living we had best be sure the memory is worthy of living in the permanance of others.

HEALTH OF BODY AND MIND

Health, all of its own self, seems to be a great contributor to contentment. Of course health aids in all our endeavors, but nonetheless, all by its own self, it seems that health is inescapably palpable. It defies any defining beyond the negatives of being without pain, or without undue exhaustion. We are an engine of incredible complexity yet coordination,- when we are in 'health'.

I've often wondered, and sometimes been asked, as I aged, what is most important in the achievement and maintenance of health? And my first inner response is always..'exercise'!!! In my own experience, exercise is the chief maker and protector of health. Exercise is the 'clean-up guy' that scrubs out the trash we've dragged in. The encourager of cheeriness when cheeriness happens to not be present. Perhaps exercise has taken on a mystic aura with me, a vague connector between the failings and laxness of my life and the finer object of uprightness and confidence,....and God? Can it be that although exercise is not as prayer or silent worship yet it can be part of our appreciation for our body and our life and thus as our partner in this manner it too comes into appreciation of God? Not of itself; I must quickly disclaim that; there are some arrogant stinkers fit as a fiddle by exercise. And there are 'men of the cloth', and 'women of the cloth', that would spoil my appetite at the dinner table.

Always, if we differ strongly in our heart with a person, as some readers will differ with my general attitude, then no matter what is said or done, it will not be acceptable. But if my words are read with tolerance, then my meanings will be quite understood. For words alone, lined up to the formal line of acceptance, are in my opinion not much fun to read and less fun to try and write. Like in painting, which is a similar effort to convey feeling. The painter who paints exactly will forever be outdone by the camera. And the photographer who does not catch the subtle in his lens is at best a neat recorder.

You know what I mean, for if you have gone beyond the aba dabbas, you've been frustrated more often in the effort to convey your meaning in conversing, than surprised by a harmony of full understanding. In fact, it leaves me strangely embarrassed to be understood. It seems a proper time to leave while the small rapture still lives. We fail if we attempt to saddle and ride every wildhorse of accord. And that's where maturity comes in, at any age whatever; the maturity to hang in there loose and grin. Where was I? Oh...Health, and exercise as first in line.

Of course health alone is only a word. We need food and assimilation and mental attitude. I don't know what all we need since I had no direct hand in the making of self. And so I confess that the whole system coordinated comes first in importance to health.

If we want to learn about health we can open any magazine or turn on the TV, and recieve profound contradictions that began with Adam.

No, I laugh, though wryly, at the battalion of experts who tell us so assuredly what, how, and why, regarding every facet of eating and drinking and how to draw in our breath and when to let it loose again. Greeeech..... But then, shewwwsw, they have to make a living somehow too. What in this world are we going to do with all the stream of college graduates depending upon assurance that they will never have to pick up greasy wrenches and crawl under dripping autos. Never have to drive nails on a wintery day while clinging to a ladder in a wind; or shingle roofs day upon day; or truck along all day and the next day while hoping to stay awake, hauling food coast to coast. No. Absolutely no. College at least assures a job safe from the weather and no tools beyond a laboratory. So you become an expert in something. And if the opening appears, you become an expert in telling people how to live. Apparently people need to be told by experts about everything from pre-conception right on through to the opening of death's door.

Unavoidably there will be opposition. Like in the art of eating. God does seem to intend that we get born, pretty adamant on that score, and once born there will be a parent in the offing who knows that a baby's mouth is preformed to close around a nipple and suck.

You don't see a niche in that plan for an expert to lurk and pop out with contradictories. At least I can't see any. But there is. There are. And supporting them are grave minds off somewhere distant, building a better substance for that little trusting, yearning-to-suck mouth with the built in attention-getting horn that outblasts a police siren, yet this natural science of eating is distorted by complications and institutions out of all proportion to need, or to common sense.

I keep close tabs on the results of all these mentioned departments of life and death and pertainings, for I attend a study on human conditions once each week at a local laboratory named Super Market. This has been a continuing interest and employment that I've attended with attention for lo these past eighty years.

It began at the not so tender age of fourteen in the neighborhood food market of Mutual Stores. A minor chain store group. We served the easy walking area, as did other such markets. The Mutal store was lodged in one side of what must have been a building designed to serve the canal boaters as well as the rural neighborhood of the previous age. The canal still flowed along just down the bank, flowed under the immediate bridge and went away yonder for some forgotten cause, since now it served almost entirely for pleasures naturally attached to gentle old canals.

Our building housed the grocery, adjoining a butcher shop which had been the saloon. Canal boating it seemed, had inspired frequent saloons. You needn't have complete senses to guide a flatboat pulled by a mule or two. Without a stimulant, that flatboating could bore the head off a wooden Indian.

We carried complete grocery supplies, including feed for chickens. We were a store of twelve feet wide by thirty feet long with a back storage room somewhat shorter. We storekeepers worked from behind a counter running down the right side. Canned goods, and packaged, ranged both sidewalls. One end abutted an ice chest holding tubs of lard and butter, cheese and eggs. Milk was delivered to homes daily from farm dairies. Milk came in bottles returned daily and rewashed. Cream rose on the raw unhomogenized milk. It was cow's milk, being drawn by a squeezing, pulling motion of the cows teats by the unwashed hands of farmers and family. It tasted like milk. It was good. I speak of the origin of milk because I've read that city kids may be dismayed upon learning of this connection with cow and milk.

If mild improvements had been made in cleanliness, and tests had been made of the cow's health, we would today be drinking real cows' milk and spreading real butter upon our bread and drinking real buttermilk and these very real little pleasures would even today be known and enjoyed by one and all free-born Americans. Amen.

What has gone wrong? Don't we dare return to a good thing of the past and improve upon it without altering the soul of that former good thing?

DOWN WITH UP AND UP WITH DOWN

Our store was run by a young man with slicked hair who closely observed the female customers as they passed out of the door into the daylight. I practiced this too. Which did me no good whatever yet urged repeated attention. I worked after school until six o'clock and Saturday until nine o'clock. Two and a half dollars per week. Customers came in and stood about waiting their turn. They might say 'a bottle of Heinz ketchup.' You walked down to the end of the counter crossed over, walked back to beside the entrance door, where the ketchup was shelved, returned and laid it down. The customer might say 'a jar of peanut butter.' Peanut butter was shelved alongside of the ketchup. The manager was bolder and would say as he picked up the ketchup, 'what next?' and in a lucky haul come back with these items. It was touch and go all through.

We had loose potatoes and onions, sugar and chicken feeds. Flour both packaged and loose. Coffee loose, and we ground it. Tea, black or Orange Pekoe, loose. I can still smell it now, nice clean outdoor's smell, brittle, sun dried. Cookies in a row of glass fronted boxes. I liked weighing out cookies for I might slip one into my pocket. It would go through the pocket for pockets never lasted, but it would lodge at my gartered short baggy knee-pants. Once I was set to cleaning the little glass doors of those cookie boxes and I garnered perhaps a dozen cookies and had to walk carefully until I was sent out to deliver an order in my express wagon. I ate them all then and was disappointed. They were not really satisfying. Actually, the cookies were lousy imitations for homemade cookies.

Imitation flavors, in the early times of man trying to copy nature, or copy God, were generally not fit to feed to an iron horse. I suspect those imitation flavors sickened a lot of people.

We had oranges during their season. Walnuts and Brazil nuts in season. A big strong black man dealt somewhat with us. He might be a bit drunk. He came in, looked at the Brazil nuts and said beligerantly to me, 'What's them called?' By sheer luck I knew that while they were 'called' nigger toes they properly were Brazil nuts. I said 'Brazil nuts.' It nettled him; he wanted to hear nigger toes and then he could get mad. The manager caught it and said sharply, 'He told you, Brazil nuts.' It was dropped. We had two black families as I recall. My father said to never use the word nigger. Always say Negro. Now its black and white. Neither very appropriate.

I wonder. If Lincoln had lived and managed to put through his drafted plan of paying purchase price for all black persons to be removed to a new territory on the coast of Africa which he had been assured of being open for purchase..... I wonder. He believed there would never be peaceful justice here. Lincoln was unusual. I think he would have made a good fellow to sit around with, jawing, exchanging thoughts. He had them. Essentially that is exactly the fellow who worked the country those terrible years when families killed one another. From a photo just after the war, he had died many times.

In my mind's eye of memory, I compare that face of Lincoln with the huge grin of Eisenhower riding down victory lane of New York

City. They were both ambitious men. How differing ambitions can be.

That was the common pattern of a neighborhood food store of that earlier period. We carried corn flakes and shredded wheat; that was it. Rolled oats and corn meal for hot cereal. Yes, there was room for improvement. Customers should have gathered their own supplies off the shelves. It didn't make sense to stand in front of a shelf containing Crisco and wait while a clerk walked down and over and up in back of you and carried it back and then you say 'and pickles' right next to it. But always there is room for improvement. Also there often is room to let good things ride. Like milk from cows, without remanufacturing it to suit some damned, and I thoughtfully wonder to what extent I really mean damned, some damned beaurocrat and probably a slew of them. Queered the whole cow and milk industry rather than just check cows for tuberculosis. I wonder if we shouldn't devise an effigy of stupidity rank, not stinking stupidity and mount it on a solid base where the wee ones would see it, get used to recognizing what it looks like. Hold a national contest for the most likely rendition. My own mental picture is a fellow with a kind of smirking smile that looks like it holds a mouthfull of tobacco juice and is ready to spit. It seems to be the likeness of a fellow in high office that registers with me. A fellow hiding a joke that he and his buddies are privy to and will laugh at when you turn your back.

I walk now around in the laboratory of the modern food market and I'm moving around among human trees. I recall when my younger height of 5'10 1/2" carried me along as above common height. We had occasional higher fellows but not common. Now even short people are taller than I. And huge! I wonder. Are they as strong as their bulk advertises them to be? 'It's the hormones' we say. They put it in the meat and milk and soda crackers, they put hormones in the damned ocean and they've got the whole damned planet hormoned into the insanity of shooting people off into space and actually thinking that's a good idea. Really. Can you sit down a moment and think about that? Dare you?

Here we are. Born with legs and feet and we strive to jump three feet straight up in the air and can't. Why is that? I mean, if, as the top man of 'space mission', or a near the topmost man declares, 'the human mind conceives of exploring space so it's right that we do so'. You see the state of this self-named 'human mind', to think that what it thinks shall be open to the doing thereof? It has got to be the hormones. For obviously that sort of mind is highly intelligent or they would never shoot themselves, or better, a willing bystander, off into space and yet not usually kill him. It takes brilliant thinking and doing. But it can't think worth beans on the basic, the common sense level. If it could, if this sort of hormone tonic-fed mind could stand on the ground and think, common sense think: 'Now here I stand and I wonder what in tarnation that moon really is made of. Would it grow tomatoes? If we got in a bind and really needed tomatoes would it grow them? Or, for that matter, would it be good for us in any way whatever? And if so, might it not seem strange that God who made us didn't give us the clear means to go up there and visit? Would he make it so hard, and using money that surely would find other needs, if he had meant us to just go on up there? He meant us to walk and to run and to jump over a small brook. And to dance, for little kids dance. All these things are apparent. But to go on up to the moon?

Maybe everything we can think of does not imply a thing waiting for us to do. What would we gain, above what would we lose, by jaunting off to the moon? It can't favor more that a few at great cost. Now would that be fair of our Father?

And what about all the other things the human mind can think of? Things possibly good and things otherwise; should they all bear the effort of doing? Or might it also be that even the great thoughts that come out of our superior minds come under the laws of making wise, distinctly God approved choices of rejecting, as well as accepting? Might we not use our minds in search of encouraging greater cooperation among nations? Might such things be worthy of our greatness of mind? Might we buckle down and do our utmost to distribute some of the waters that could so very greatly aid people dying of need for good water? And might we work strong on a really efficient composter for every home so that we stop that so highly unintelligent waste of our waste, and waste of our water tables?

Golly whiz! but there is sure a parcel of things that we actually might succeed in bettering and so do good for many people. Maybe even foreigners. Enemies cranking out stores of mass destruction. Persons of inferior intellect; living off little patches of land. Imagine. No autos. No highway systems. None to speak of at least.

Let's chuck that idea of hormoning everything into bigger and bigger. What for? Are those hulking food store habitues more capable than the Japanese?

There's a whole lot to health. Almost all of it clearly visible to a non-hormones mind. Babies should be fed by their mothers. God put anti disease things in Mom's milk and it will aid baby to remain healthy. Little children should be kept away from the artificially grown, prepared, packaged food substitutes. Can we expect to grow and sustain natural people with unnatural food?

Mothers should not need to go to work away from home. Parents should have much time to venture into spaces they have never known existed. We should start moving toward large plots where families can supply much of their own natural foods. Ventures should be made in getting systematic exercises daily. I will speak of this directly. Ventures into getting enough sleep and rest find that health prospers from it. There would be less sickness if we killed TV and went to bed. Ventures in making one's own shoes. Did you ever hear of the 'space' shoe you can form of soft fabric and rubber cement. Form right on your feet? They are the best shoe you can't buy. But it takes time. Do you bake your own bread? No time? Yes, it takes near four hours. Not so much in the mixing but in the raising and baking.

Last evening, I baked one loaf of bread. My loaf weighs three and a half pounds. I bake it in a flat bottomed mixing bowl. The little child-in-semi-residence of whom I spoke comes in twice daily to ask for a piece of my bread. She doesn't want butter on it, just plain. A big slice. She thinks I should make a loaf for them to keep, so she wouldn't need to ask for it. I can give exact directions for making a loaf of bread. I helped mix the dough for Gramma when I was a boy. She had begun kneading dough for their family of seven when she was six. I recall her speaking of this. I can tell how to make a good plain bread and you might like it. Or might not. Bread is like that. Write me, with a SASE and I'll send it to you.

We hear of eating heavy of meat. The Atkins diet? Shew. There's nothing new about it. I recall immediately one such family. Boy, did they ever buy the meat. Heavy, strong people, parents and kids. Not too good on longevity or general health. But that proves nothing. I think a nice mix is best. Although, I don't feel easy about eating eggs and chicken from chickens that don't have room to flap their wings. I see one such chicken raiser reduced his cages from nine per cell to seven. He says they now can flap their wings. You see what sensitive people we are becoming? Another chicken chap raised 'cage-free' chickens; they are in one great chicken house and they carpet the floor solidly. Another assures 'free roaming' for his hens. Oh? How do they gather the eggs from a huge flock of free roamers? We had a dozen hens free in a fenced yard and they found endless things to peck at, but they were not free roaming.

That term of 'freedom' clings fast to our life. There are strings of restraint attached to every heart beat of a molecule. If you want something simulating freedom, get into your upwards of 200 horse powers and launch it on a highway. With those wild horses raging to cut loose, you have just inches of freedom plus needs for your full share of luck. And that's one more aspect of the health issue.

To get back to exercise, I will relate, condensed, all that I've learned of it in eighty years of close attention and a flood of exertion.

First, there are many kinds of body exercise and many ways to do them. They all entail the alternate contracting and relaxing of muscle. One consideration is when to exercise. During most of my eighty years of conscious exercise, I have exercised after supper. It was most convenient, and contrary to common advise, lots of us do our exercise soon after supper. I suspect that digestion may delay to accomodate the demand for blood. I don't think it would be the best time for running or hard swimming. But neither is it good just before eating. Early in the morning might do for light flexing. I think not for vigorous and prolonged movement. I think animals go along with that.

Where? As close to where you sleep and eat as is practical. My first gym was a self-built 12 x 12 foot cabin, or shack. That unheated cabin in northern NJ served me for gym and sleeping for six years. It gets cold in the north hills of NJ. Often to zero, twice to 24 below.

I had no fixed period of exercise. It ran from a half to a whole hour. I think this is probably a good, and sufficient time to daily clean up the system. I worked steadily alternating from a heavy exercise to a lighter one, never pausing unless I began to feel ill. I believe that worked as well, if not better, than any single form of movement, like running, or walking.

All my exercises used resistance. Mostly solid iron dumbells and barbells. For many years I started with fifteen full chinning of the bar. Second, fifteen full pressups between roman rings. These sets of movements required a little hop to get up to them. So they never were 'cheater' movements. I felt that my muscles had a certain range of motion so it seemed more important to exercise that full movement than to bring vanity and competitiveness even into a process of health and strength.

I believe I stated that unfortunate circumstance from the age of three through ten had so injured my original health and vigor that I was distinctly behind normal and afflicted with bouts of joint and muscle pain from rheumatic fever. Along with the nervous disorder aptly termed St. Vitus Dance. A jerking, twitching of all the body at times. I could almost control it but it was a strain to do so for long, and when the needs for release were most pronounced, I would try to find a place where I could release the demons and just go into a twitching, jerking passion. That would relax me fairly well for a while. If I was discovered at such a time, it brought deep shame and the knowledge that I would be unjustly judged for it. I knew two other boys in highschool with rheumatic fever, and mild muscle jerking, but both of these boys were muscular and well developed. One died in mid twenties; the other in mid thirties. They had bed and medical treatment. I felt obliged to keep silent and never was actually diagnosed as having rheumatic fever until years later. We simply were not in a position to have an ailing child. Yet my grandmother's brother was a doctor. Isn't that strange. My heart was damaged and I fainted easily and lacked endurance. And, bluntly, I was ill for those seven years. And ill treated. My sister, 19 months my senior, and I. And our father was a medically induced addict to narcotics. My sister lived to about 90 and I was born in January of 1910. So if I still live then my age is arithmatic. And for a long while my heart has shown no damage. During my prime years, my pulse was under forty. That can be good and also can be bad.

From age ten, our grandmother came into the family and boy oh boy, where did that little old lame woman learn to cook every last and little food so good. I never solved her system nor understood her knowledge. And she knew how to have a mixed diet all through the week every week. Yet, my body couldn't respond. I had been mashed down too far and too long. Not until I turned seventeen and simply took charge of myself, against all the disapproval of family, did I burst free from my prison of suppression.

Do you not see why I am so rabid against any least dominance of one human over another? Simplified: infringe not upon another's natural rights; permit no infringement upon one's own rights. Individuality is basic to health of body, mind and soul. Individuality is basic to sound friendship. I probably would put myself in the way of death to protect your independence even if I actively disliked you. That is part of pride and treasure of one's individuality. Dear Person, we are made individual by our Father, God-All-Mighty! Do we dare be dominated meekly? Shall we let any or all government and materialism counter God's so evident laws? Shall we servilely aid in that evil by our quiet submission?

As stated, and surely repeatable here, exercise, combined with freedom from the restraint, the literal imprisonment, of school, unblocked the dam that had so long cut off the free flow of life and growth. The relief was evident within two weeks.

My first attempts to exercise were blunders, practiced in the cellar. I nailed up a little chinning bar between the ceiling joists but there was insufficient head room, also I sensed that weights were needed. I put sand in a burlap bag, but such an indefinite object offered little aid. I began at once to plan the building of a small cabin and my father granted me the use of the end of the chicken yard, almost against the neighbor's barn.

There was a lumber yard a couple of blocks around the corner. They had such big piles of boards and my needs were relatively small. So I went over there by the aid of darkness and pulled out three boards and with considerable discomfort hauled them home on my bony boy shoulders. Two trips was all I could endure. Next morning Daddy saw the trend of things and took an opposing view. I agreed to send them the value of the theft. However, to determine that value, I must deduct self delivery, and the pain of that delivery. This quite reduced the board value. In the end, I decided to give them all my future trade in construction of the cabin, so what I had taken resolved to a free sample. I suppose many a life of crime is induced by such unseasoned reasoning.

The cabin went up. It had no choice. Twelve feet square, board floor, three windows and a door. All open regardless of weather. I framed in a canvas bunk in one corner. It served two years, with a cotton quilt for mattress, and a sheet and cotton quilt for covers. I added plenty of newspaper bottom and top and probably that served to sustain life. Later I added a horse blanket which I discarded a year ago. I had, for reasons I can't recall, determined upon a Spartan regimen as most beneficial to health. So I wore only pants and shirt. A head cold resulted and partly mended but remained in its half strength until spring.

Gradually I accumulated iron weights, and they have remained my favored apparatus even into this day. I once surely had seven hundred pounds of barbells and solid iron dumbells. With a chinning bar and small Roman rings, I see no need for costly apparatus which needs space and adjusting of resistance. Iron weights will serve a feeble old granny or a burgeoning young buck and never wear out.

They are not alluring; they make no vague promises. They even look foreboding. However, we never need to choose a weight which is strenuous. It is our choice.

People exercise for various reasons, some reasons even being opposing to others. A most common reason, which also is the poorest reason, is to make big muscles. Isn't that on a keel with driving more car than we need? When I pose that question, I look directly at myself, for it applied. If I could have achieved it I would have grown muscles so big they would have got in the way of each other. And probably would have owned three cars and each excessive in its class.

It was stupid. Short of reasoning. Desirous of admiration. We never can know the so-pleasing feeling of being satisfied as long as we focus and yearn for more, more, bigger, better, prettier. Most of our ambitions are made of vanity and greed. Such sorry displacement of good character and kindness.

I firmly support a full system of achieving and retaining health, strength, and appearance. I have much confidence in the ability of health to improve one's usefulness to oneself and to others. I support the gaining of as much strength as results from a wise course of living and exercising. I admire attractiveness of form without reservation. But any such gains should be the result of one's living habits, and not the goals.

I believe that if one is capable of exercising about a half to a full hour each evening after supper, or any time most convenient,

I believe that it must be a wise investment. The results can soon be judged by our inner feeling. We should gain a feeling of health and peacefulness. We must not stress ourself to exhaustion which is not refilled over night. Incidentally, this test of overnight recovery is the best way to determine if we overdo our exertion. I can't approve the method of going one's limit today, then two or three days to recover. This places the emphasis upon performance and not upon health. Nature would approve a sensible tiredness, a tiredness which strangely feels comforting. If we give reasonable, not fetish, attention to all aspects of general health, the result will be elevation of health, inward and outward, and distinct vitalizing of spirit. I believe, without any extensive proof, that wise exercise would go far to defeat depression and anxiety.

Wisely we will be content with moderate gains for this we can achieve. Much better to be content with what our nature is granted than to spend life trying to excell in things of no real worth.

Most systems place too much emphasis upon outward appearance. The theory is that if we labor for appearance there will naturally result inward gain. The opposing theory is that if we labor for inner health, the outward appearance will gain as a sort of bonus. Life is a tricky system of balance. We practice it unthinkingly in every detail throughout. It is best to be conscious of our inward condition and the outward appearance will be what it must be.

We may wonder just how to perform our exercise. Surely we are aware, even if we give it no conscious thought, that we all move a little differently. Slow, quick, jerky, smooth, and endless combinations of movements. We can regulate our movements somewhat, although I suspect from my long observations, that few of us make much effort in this direction. I have had to, for the St. Vitus caused me to be so conscious of my movements that I doubt there was any natural movement left in me. So I watched other people. Watched how they moved and what seemed to be the result. Truly it was somewhat bewildering. Even today I wonder if a person's general muscular structure is the result of their manner of movement, or is it the reverse.

One person, from childhood, is strongly muscled, thick muscled, often rather solid in movement. Another, slender muscled, seems joined with the character of the person. Is there research to conclude that a person with a given body structure is going to have a linked mental nature? React in a foreseen manner? I suspect this may be something true infinitely. Then who is to praise or blame for the resulting person? You see, if we let our searching wander back along the paths of interlives, we may really find at least some predestination. And if we conclude with this, then will it not be quite more than merely interesting when the 'day of reckoning' greets us? But that will, of course, be just. In this term of our prekindergarten how unwise and distinctly incautious we are to judge the interior of anyone, even our dear spouse sitting across the table with coffee cup part raised, regarding us enigmatically. Just what is this dear spouse really thinking and what part is the result of configuration?

However, such idle conjecture is of some worth, for it halts the judgement of a person down to the core of the soul, preventing us from relegating to hell those not destined to burn. It seems we must read the primer our nature provides.

Regarding the physical development, and movement given us at birth, my recall brings back one boy who distinctly was in a class of muscular integrity so remarkable that I have never again seen its like.

He was shorter than average and would top out at 5'6". However, he clearly was conscious of, and in control of, every movement at every moment. This was more than a mere stolidity. It was an apparent conscious directing of the body in motion and repose. Even the eyes. Even the toes, for mark this. Some of us poorer boys wore 'Boyscout' shoes. They were simple, full height shoes of moderately firm leather. Very plain, soft toed. He was a neat boy and tried to polish his shoes. And, to mark the closeness of my effort to understand movement, I observed that his shoes would soon acquire individual bulges where each toe obviously was curled or lifted upward with each step. You see, even his toes were being flexed in their full range, not just in the more common downward clenching move, or no move at all. The shape of a person's calf is influenced by the movement of the toes. His calf was a form for girls to admire, and for a boy like me to envy.   I never saw that boy make an unaware movement. Every move was an exercise, smooth, fluid and apparently under slight tension. Catlike, yet even exceeding the cat. People would come to games when he was in highschool just to watch him move. I've watched quite a number of trained athletes, performerers, beautifully coordinated in their acts, but never have I seen one other who was at all times performing an act.

I spoke of this with a man well acquainted with physical culture, a world record holder for perfect development, and a national trainer of injured army veterans. His only remark was that such obvious tension could not be practiced long for it results in severe headache whenever it has been attempted. I agreed with him. Except in this one case.

This boy, standing 5'6" x 170 lbs, one year in college football scored second in national touchdowns. To this day I have no established movement. I generally prefer a loose, almost dangling movement. It makes me feel relaxed in my mind. And that raises another memory.

This was of a young black lifter. At 198 x 5'9" he held the world's light-heavyweight amateur lifting title. And was he ever loose in movement; not sloppy loose, just so nicely lubricated loose that he could lie down across a few seats between lifts and grin at the spectators. A likeable fellow. Jim Thorpe too was able to lie down and nap between football halves, and he was quite in his one and only class of natural athletes. But back to this lifting champion, John Davis.

At a strength meet, the M.C. was Sam Olmstead, mid-sixties and with a body that would delight any mid-twenties fellow. Sam was one of the rare men who could chin the bar with one hand while weighing above 160. He related, that while watching a group of lifters training he had mentioned the bar chinning feat to John Davis and John had said: 'I can chin it one hand, Sam.' Sam was amazed to see this finely proportioned 200 lb. young man draw himself up with his right hand, and then the same with his left. Then to really put the squash on it he took a 50 lb dumbell in his left hand and drew himself up with his right. That equals a 250 lb man chining with one hand. How can one person so excel, and there be no visible reason?

There are physical strengths so outstanding that one may well look forward to that future when once again we will all have control and strength which rarely exists now. Like the German strong man of early 1900's. Arthur Saxon. Scrupulously honest, among those who are not scrupulously honest. The bent-press lift is a movement wherein the lifter hoists the barbell to the shoulder, holding it there balanced upon the one hand, and then with an explosive movement, drops down and thrusts upward and, if successful, rises with the bar held aloft above his head. Try it with a broom and try to imagine doing this with 300 lb. Very rare is the man who has succeeded with 300.

Saxon, during one engagement, performed this lift with 301 lbs six times each day throughout the week. His official record was 371 lbs. Then a Scottish strong man questioned his honesty, saying that Saxon, at 200 lbs, could not possibly bent-press 371 lbs. So Saxon, one Sunday, arrived at the Scots' home. They put together a barbell, with additional weights tied to the ends of the bar until it felt right to Saxon. He shouldered the mass and dropped under it. A small plate broke loose as Saxon rose to full stretch. The Scot enthusiastically conceded the dropped weight, for the hard part had been done. They weighed the mass; it was a full 406 lbs.

When we see human potential so excelled, we well may gasp and wag our head, for we have nothing to parallel it in common life. Like the fellow who strung a slackwire over Niagara River below the falls and not only walked it, but according to the report, wheeled a trusting soul over in a wheelbarrow. No room there for a balancing pole. It was also recorded that he walked it blindfolded. This latter may hit a negative, but consider: if we are in good condition, are we not able to stand in pitch darkness and not fall down? Then with reasonable extension might not a chap simply walk over a wire if his sense of balance was supurb?

But return to earth, and simply the application of exercises to one's life with the intention of inducing better health, and let any gains appear as they might.

First, I recommend exercising alone. We need to concentrate upon the engaged muscle group. We need to feel the movement.

Don't concern yourself about how fast or slow you perform. Try various ways and be assured there are many others trying to find their own most effective way. Keep moving from one exercise to the next. Just as in walking, you don't stop, for it interrupts the goodness of a steady exertion.

If you need to be told where you keep your various muscle groups, or need to be told what moves each group can make, then buy something by someone who has found he can sell such a common knowledge. Otherwise, experiment. Perform each move to its full. Full contraction of the muscle or group and full contraction of the counter group. For you realize that we only have contraction of movement so we always must have a counter contraction to return the movement. In some cases, such as squats, the squatting motion does not use the opposing group. For your weight supplies the motive power, but be assured the opposing muscles do exist and are used in other moves.

What intensity of contraction should we apply? Don't damage the muscle with too severe a contraction. You don't need to forcefully contract if you don't want to. Experiment. Don't be troubled if today you know that you have found the ideal schedule and then tomorrow find that it doesn't satisfy as it had yesterday. Be prepared to change, to suit the desires or needs of the day.

Now, how many repetitions are best?

It seems the present science is to do ten 'reps', then pause and repeat. This is supposed to make bigger 'mass'. From my retarded view, I say forget mass. Stick with health. With function. Making mass feels best to you? Then make mass. But try to retain that mass. You can't. It isn't natural. But health can be rather well retained, and with luck right up to near the end. The good feeling of health. I still have it.

Then the 'reps'? Arthur Saxon favored 5 to 7 for making muscle; 2 or 3 for strength, once the muscle has been gained. Then there were, perhaps still are, the wrestling groups of India. They had a reputation for their ability, although I had not heard of them touring this country.

They lived closely, small groups, eating mostly rice and chicken. Like one or two chickens a day. They seldom weighed over two hundred, and were said to have a smooth layer of fat over their body. They would lie in cold mountain streams for a period each day. Maybe partly for the thought that the water spirit entered them? And they had six exercises which they daily performed. The reps were from about seven or eight hundred times to two-thousand for the squats.

It must have built good muscle. I think it was a Hungarian wrestler, big man, 250 or more, who was curious so he went over to India and sought out the location of a known group. It was their supper time. The Hungarian wanted to wrestle. The Indian leader weighed 200. He said, 'My brother will wrestle you.' The brother weighed 160 or 165. Pretty insulting to big man. It lasted three quick successive 'pinfalls'. The big man was thrown three times. So, was their training method good?

I knew of those who advocated 15 reps, as I did, and those of 18 and of 35 reps. Or 12. We are individual.

These 'Iron Man' contests of today, which include 'iron women' too. Now there is a grind. Why do people do such things? Is it fun? If so it must be a fun different from mine. It lasts too dang long, too depleting. I don't believe it's a good idea even if they like it. It puts the body at risk, as if it were of little value weighed against our search for dangerous thrills. It overrides the Source of our body and life; quite overlooks our Creator and even any premise of a purpose accompanying the gift of life. Really, it marks an absence of mental growth; hardly a circumstance to admire. Probably if we do respond with admiration we place ourself farther down the line of mental growth than the adventurers. They do show courage, even though ill placed.

Probably I've sufficiently expressed my high regard for exercise, full body exercise, with first attention upon health. But one specific form of exercise comes to mind and the reason for it may be of value to us all: that is to exercise the neck, the muscles surrounding the neck.

Some long way back, possibly the Greeks during their period of concentration upon the human form, it was observed that as the neck was made 'round' the mind functioned more clearly. We don't usually associate mental improvement with general body and health improvement. But shouldn't we? In a moderate way. For how can we seperate the one from the other? And while the scholar may acquire more exotic knowledge, does that assure the scholar's mental function itself is superior?

When we exercise the neck, we must flex the two carotid arteries, running up each side of the neck to supply the brain with ample blood; we must thoroughly flex and knead and in general exercise them and how can that avoid aiding those arteries toward full flowing? The fact that these two arteries are in a location to provide flexing is not by chance, don't hesitate to credit a purpose in every part and function of our so marvelous body. Hallow ourself. Not with self aggrandizement but with awe that our Father entrusts a Self with us.

THE ETERNAL PEACE OF NOW

All that I have written of in this book has been engaged in the activity of violence. Yet, my life is directed toward peace. The peace that David seems to imply in the Psalm 23.

We must counter destructive activity with an equivalent degree of violence. A dangerously speeding auto needs the violence of brakes to halt it. The English ravaging of India was halted by the violence of Gandhi's resistance.

But the pure peace which we can only conjecture must be in the non-violent timeless eternity of Now. The non-material point where future and past meet. I realize that we cannot achieve fully this sense of peace, a worldly nirvana, but we can individually guide our daily and hourly life by its ideal. We can consciously learn to take whatever comfort and peace and joy from the moment of Now that our situation offers. If we do this we immediately elevate our existence. We get it up out of its small agonies which too often are agonies of our own manufacture. Like, we may be delayed and the delay seems unbearable because so much hinges upon it, so we choose to think things which add to the burden even though we have the power to think things to lighten it.

Life demands activity, and I surely would not want it to be other, but when we live at the center of our activity, we can inwardly smile and observe what we are doing. And have done. And are about to do. If we are at the non-disturbing point of mental peace, we can enjoy doing the dishes, take pleasure in our movements, be quite childlike. Breathe in the situation. Taste the day, and in short we are not obliged to suffer just to prove that we are aware of our life.

This is reducing life to it's poverty of exterior wealth. Oh yes. Exactly. And thereby we learn to live in the Now...where true life lives. Not where this world we have devised lives, but where the world of peace and our Father's love envelop us. There is no bad situation which cannot be made worse by drawing on the evil of past and future. There is no situation which cannot be made better by confining it to the peace of Now. That's Faith. In the Peace of Now, much of our burden vanishes.

TO BUILD A HOME

I don't know how it could be denied that we are each a unique individual, though of one kind. Being individuals it seems fitting that we should be self-sustaining. In quite rare environments that might require just enough awareness to grab fruit and get it into our mouth and lie down to sleep when tired. I guess with our common nature we would procreate if we were born rocks.

But most all of us live in circumstances that strongly demand we shall honor the three basic needs, which include shelter. Not shelter of caves for there were never enough caves for that ill thought term of 'cave man'. Thin populations and adequate foraging made the cave desirable and those who lived in caves left their bones somewhat protected from weather and beasties until they got covered over with ages of ashes and whatever that age offered of trash. There had to be trash or they were not human. I see the moon shooters want to return to that site of their trash. Add to it. Spend an embarrassing money on hand before the next largess is apportioned. Children must play, no matter their age or ingenuity. Otherwise they would no longer be children.

What I would suggest is that every family-man had reason to acquire a home. A house of some sort. So it is quite born into us to be able to build us a home. It rounds out the basic man. So why doesn't every family simply build themselves a home? With all the passing of time it seems that the knowledge and skill would be available to every family one notch above imbecility. Even a beaver cuts down small trees and builds a log house and he doesn't even have a hammer or saw. Just teeth and ingrained vision of a log house.

We have numbers of obstructions toward home building today. One is that persons have seen fit to lay claim to excessive land areas and of course the laws, which are basically protective of wealth (what else would they protect), protect the land holdings. And if you think it should be easy to go with purchase money in hand and express your need to a land owner, 'one acre of land, please, and here is my purchase money', then you are not experienced in homesite searching.

There are impediments to finding that one acre requisite to building your home. Like the need for access and the limit of the owner's road frontage. Or, if the owner does want to sell off a tract, there may be very costly requirements of roads and streets and paving which have been diddled into the local laws for reasons not quite available for review. And so it may take several years of search, as was our experience, or you may give up and buy or rent a trailer patch where a privacy of sorts can be secured.

It is unjust. Unkind. And nothing much being done about it. Also there is water access and waste disposal and road maintenance for the accomodation of that alluring devastator, the auto. I surely would hope to see this injustice quickly righted with the coming of the Voterbox. If we, the voiceless mass of workers, do not go after that opportunity of Democracy with the sweeping power of a tidal wave, then I will have to give up on the experiment of humankind and run for political office to keep me away from the illusion of common sense.

Yes, it can be very hard to find an acre of land. And today the prices are far above realizm. It does look like there could be a tumble in those inflated prices before we can struggle out of the debt we are plunging into. So if you can put money aside now, you should do so. And seriously, we may achieve the true democracy, which will bring land accessability.

Assuming you do now have a plot or will find one, it would be nice if it has a south slope. Or is flat. But be cautious of a northern slope. The north puts stress upon our nature.

Although I've been building for over sixty years, in some stage of construction, and building quite a lot of furniture too, still I can't here say much of building detail. There are welters of books on the subject. Some of them offer sound advise for a worker builder. Some are too primitive to be practical.

I strongly advise building into the earth in some fashion. If you can bulldoze a broad shelf across the face of a south slope it is a fine thing to do. It is reported that several feet down the earth temperature throughout our country is around 50 to 55 degrees. So if we can make substantial contact with the earth at that temperature, it is an aid in tempering the climate of our home both winter and summer.

Our own home is about 2200 square feet of floor space on two equal levels. The bottom level contacts the earth through the slab with wood floor, and the rear masonary wall. On hot days I have this bottom floor open nights for cooling and closed days to retain the cool. At times it is too cool so I must open the doors to let the summer heat come in to temper it.

We heat with wood, with gas for backup or if we wish to leave in the winter. Wood has been condemned by government backed authority as being a pollutant. Wood smoke settles as wood ash dust and is a fertilizer. So wood, where it's plentiful, is next to the sun in acceptable heat.

A working family's most used room is the kitchen. Visitors congregate in the kitchen if any work is going on there. It seems best to make a generous and well favored room of the kitchen. A few lounge chairs, maybe a couch or sofa, and a good sized general purpose table. Small bedrooms and baths. A pantry with laundry. Attached deck or porch. A pool may be good. About four feet deep, no shallow and deep end. A pool can be a problem but also can be worth the trouble.

A garden fertilized with family compost will help financially and in health. A composting devise made of fiberglass will take all household waste and leaves and make fine garden food without waste. Probably reduce sickness. Chickens and eggs are good. In proper circumstances a cow or goat.

A good house can be made of masonary, poured into slip forms where you pour only eight inches or so each time around. Sand and cement, about one cement to eight of sand, or clay, or soil, makes a good wall, eight inches thick. You can do it with a book or so to guide. Get started and you may do the entire job. It's our right and it is a good thing to do.

If you build a plain rectangular home and wonder about the proportion which apparently is pleasing to our common eye,- for some reason I won't probe into, you might consider the 'golden section' ; roughly, the width is three fifths (.625%) of the length.

There is so much I would say, but it seems that it might not be required. I have intended that the little book should have a need. Scarcely in answer to a universal request, yet in response to a universal need, for it is a commune of one earnest human to the many other earnest persons. The attempt to cover the broad subject of one common but uncommonly questioning lifetime of near one century confronted a formidable problem. There simply was far too much which demanded inclusion.

There were bald facts of change and accomplishments, which gather into a literal catalog. To illustrate each event with our own experience and thought is too lengthy. Books of great length demand great research. And will rarely be widely read. I wanted a book that would be read, and sensed for some while back that I had the materials and simple writing ability to fill the book's need. So I started writing it.

I tried to indicate my convictions in a novel. I wrote it twice. As a long time avid reader I knew that it was a good novel and suitable for a 'Christian Publishers' printing. So I spent 79 dollars on a Christian web site. It added to my suspicion of commercial Christianity. If they had bought and sold it, I might have softened my opinion. I was fortunate.

When I found the open but overlooked proof, of God's literal presence recorded in the Bible, I knew my modest, and at times crudely, written book was assured. It would be written, and read, for it is true of things which the weaker side of our nature is everlastingly, bulldogedly determined to keep buried under the thousand of years of raw greed. And I am of the conviction, today, we who are past the age of existing under the stink of rotting morality and honored greed, that we constitute a force that shall prove too right to be held down by the desperate attack of greed. I believe we are a force which will again raise the shining goal of life in the joy of God's eternal comfort.

I began to wonder just how much writing around and about I had actually done on this subject of life. So I attempted to measure its length, by typed line, ten letters and spaces to the inch and like certain other quantities it was unbelievable.

My typing paper comes in reams of 500 sheets. The typing ribbon is wound on a spool 2 1/2 inches in diameter. That little spool of tape is 500' long. A football field is 300 feet long. I try to estimate how many tapes and how many reams of paper I've used in the past four years of writing toward this little book. I try to be conservative in my estimate so I'll say that I've used forty spools of tape, though I suspect it might be fifty. Reams of paper are commensurate.

So, forty tapes measure 20,000 feet. A mile is 5,280 feet. Three and three-quarters miles. Ten taps of the keys per inch. Nawww......Ridiculous. Nearly four miles of pecking, ten pecks to the inch? What a penance that would be. Yet that's an indication of what writers, steady writers, will go through and then only a thin scattering of them can make a living at it.

Yet there are persons who possess one billion dollars. Forty-thousand a year income is pretty rich to my thinking. If you saved all forty-thousand, it would take twenty-five thousand years to save one billion. Is that possible? I don't like to know that we tolerate this kind of inequality. But we do. And then in the top level of our Government they even speak of trillion. And the rich get richer and the poor get lice.

DOWN WITH UP AND UP WITH DOWN

BRIEF REVIEW

In our past century we have done some marvelous things. However, we are unavoidably human, and therefore subject to believe that anything we do which is marvelous must also be a thing which is right.

Having no more than a working education, which today means somewhat beyond that which directed Lincoln and Washington and Franklin and such fellows, it gives me reason to pause and wonder how those lowly privileged persons were able to think so well. What was their bedrock of wisdom? And I could scarcely conclude other than that they relied heavily upon Common Sense.

So, although I constantly experiment with every wisp of my life, at the end of each day I return to my own bedrock of wisdom which is the Bible, and Common Sense.

Therefore, I would betray my own integrity, both given me at birth, and acquired quite without my will, if I did not judge my nearly full century of absorbings such life as is easily seen and otherwise quite widely advertised, if I did not make my present judgements of my findings by the bedrock of the Bible and Common Sense.

It might be quickly exclaimed, 'yeah, you mean your own view of common sense; but each of us is endowed with a personal common sense, and how will you deny or answer that?'

I won't try to answer it. Rather, I agree with it. I only hope that you use it and find it useful, as I have used mine. In this manner I strongly suspect that God has provided us to come quite together, if we do indeed honor our Common Sense.

I assume we can all agree that terrible harm has been done to our home. Our own Earth by tenant rights. We can see that our air is less clean, our water is less sweet, and our soil is distinctly, by view and analysis of its fruits, in a sickly condition and we do not know how to cure it!!

'We', and I am not foolish when I say that We includes almost all of us, and I am of that majority. But I have, by the power of reviewing my own century, withdrawn from my support of the ways we have gone and are now going and, I must reveal most strongly the one most monstrous flaw in our society and it does not happen to be a flaw which I have supported at any time. I thank the Lord for that, since I see no point at which it was of my own brilliance.

That terrible flaw in our society is the indisputable fact that this society, this great Nation, is absolutely devoid of any Eternally Shining Goal!!

By the proof of our past century, and the proof of our present inflexible direction, we do not function within the conviction of an

Everlasting Life! We literally are without any goal which extends beyond the here and the now!

We are told that our present man in power prays each morning for direction. And then supports violence as the lever to our national safety and growth. And when our so-called 'economy' falters, he uses a like wisdom and exhorts the citizenry to make more purchases to get things rolling.

If we did as a nation, function with that Shining Goal of Eternity within the full aura of God, our Father, then would we live within a working philosophy that it is better by far to defeat our fellow beings and thus gain power and profit, than it would be to earnestly give care to one another and make every effort to share, and lift the weak, not take advantage of the weak. And this sharing would extend outward from neighbor to nation aiding nation; a reversal of all our engagements.

So, briefly assessing our position and its inflexible direction and obvious intention, I flatly state that having no Shining Goal assuredly dooms this society within itself and dooms this American Nation within the world.

It seems too apparent that those Bible searchers who have for many years foreseen our nation as the great Babylon which will amaze the world by its sudden destruction, it seems that they will prove wise in their foresight.

As we continue to make ill-will among the nations, we also encourage retaliation, and the form and effectiveness of that retaliation will not be limited to using our own planes as weapons of destruction. A nation so bemused by the satanic vision of every worker driving a chariot pulled by 200 powers of horse, and thereby drawing the great bulk of the people into dependence for daily food upon continual lines of great trucks......

Meanwhile, we waste our resources of the present, and put our future into hock, while we attempt to dominate lesser nations. And the whole affair of this society is designed to enrich the rich and powerful and control the worker herd from kindergarten teachings on to our death.

We are now a nation doomed. Common Sense asserts it. The Bible asserts it. I am only one of the growing many who assert it and we know that only by swift action can it even possibly be averted. It's so utterly, vividly, evident!

God speaks in the Bible. The Bible warns that there will be a time when those who have not dedicated themselves to earnestly obeying God's precepts toward being accepted into Eternal Life within his Kingdom, that those of us who hold off from this commitment, perhaps thinking to wait for the last moment, may as well continue in their wrong ways when the cut-off point comes. And it comes without specific warning. Could it have already come? Who can say not?

As for matters of our present life, I strongly urge that we press for absolute Democracy through the Voterbox or whatever means might be more effective.

It is vital, if we continue as a living Nation, to gain complete rule of our present conduct and our future goals. I say this with hope, and some trust, that as a whole people we might prove of greater wisdom and compassion than under the dominence of the Mob Rule of the Rich and Powerful. Really, could we do less good? Are we, collectively, as ruthless as those who now dominate us? Heaven help us all if we are.

I strongly urge that we take possession of our Nation. That we reverse our insanity of ever wanting more and make great effort to do with far, far less and gain more contentment from what is clearly and rightly available.

I urge then that we eliminate all manufacture which is not truly necessary. And that all jobs be apportioned as equally as possible. Much as Roosevelt attempted, and with quick success, until the Court, backed by the cry of the rich, struck it down. A simple matter of equal sharing. Shall I think myself more worthy of life's needs than my neighbor? Heaven forbid.

That all jobs then be shared and so the work hours be cut to a fraction. That all proceeds be as equally apportioned wages. That no one shall garner a profit. That any industry, for small worker owned industries will thrive, that no industry shall retain a profit above operating needs. That any profit which may result shall be taken toward the national tax. That all money shall be labor based and thus any nation which shall adopt this may trade upon equal basis.

With labor based money our self-government will issue labor based pay for any project approved by general vote. Thus we shall have no national debt and our enterprises will be only limited by what the people deem needful.

That all lands habitable shall be made available in living sized plots and so return our nation to rural-village, which is superior, being closer to nature's edict. Any enterprise which is not tuned to nature is doomed at the outset.

The entire transportation system must be replaced by sanity as swiftly as possible. Improved rail, trolley, truck, and entirely revised auto, based upon the bicycle, as designed by B. Fuller in 1933. Of course it was squelched by the much affrighted auto maker moguls. It shamed them into messing themselves both morally and I suspect explicitly.

Education would be removed from the design of supplying workers to enrich the rich and might actually become a non system of constant education open and free and thereby a most delightful part of our lives.

Health, of course, would be simply the best we can provide and either free or so structured that all could afford it.

Religion would not be excluded from education, for it is never a dangerous subject except where badly infected by the religionists. God, our so evident Father, is never a topic to require restrictions.

Friends, Foes, and all that fall between: We have been a considerable while in residence here on this planet-earth. Whether measured accurately or not is of no consequence; it is a long while and we have an abysmal record of tenancy.

We individually grow from apparent infancy into apparent adulthood. But we do fail and fail and perpetually fail to grow in maturity. Doesn't maturity imply that we might improve in our kindness toward one another? Doesn't it imply that as we meet life's trials and griefs we might apply our responses to our neighbor no matter where our neighbor might be placed?

The mark of growth and refinement is the level of our kindness toward one another. Shall we not attempt now, for when shall a more fertile time arrive, attempt to help one another in all ways that wisely encourage help? Shall we not apply our considerable means toward processing and conveying water to all people who need water, often desperately need water? Why, by sheer muscle power we could provide ways to convey water in survival quantities and thereby make kindness a working commodity rather than a symbolic word.

Shewww.... We are humans! We are of flesh that too often pains. And souls too often bathed in tears. We are spirits that lift with a lifting glance or a lifting word and soar with a helping hand.

We have such a short while here. We each shall die either today or tomorrow. How well if we can know that we shall die in acts that shall not condemn us.

Again: The saintly man of a past generation is hoeing his garden. And a neighbor, passing by, pauses to exchange greetings. Then, as the saint resumes hoeing, the neighbor ponders him a few moments, and struck with the resulting thought, asks, 'What would you do right now if you knew that the End-time would come tomorrow?' And the saint replies, 'I would hoe my garden.'

ABOUT THE AUTHOR

Foster was born in 1910, when automobiles were rich men's toys that scared horses. He came into the world screaming, 'there's got to be a better way!' and from there on, he's been at odds with the social order. In due time he saw that he strove for the bedrock of Common Sense.

By his personal poll, he states that Common Sense would topple 77% of all human enterprise. In fact the only problem he's ever had with the wisdom of Common Sense is obeying it.

For a serious guy he seems to thrive on humor, finding it lurking in 81% to 84% of every situation; though he cautions that humor is not always to be laughed at.

www.ingramcontent.com/pod-product-compliance
Lightning Source LLC
Chambersburg PA
CBHW030320290526
45785CB00001B/443